D1716652

AKEMAN STREET

Moving Through Iron Age and Roman Landscapes

Tim Copeland

The
History
Press

First published 2009

The History Press
The Mill, Brimscombe Port
Stroud, Gloucestershire, GL5 2QG
www.thehistorypress.co.uk

British Library Cataloguing in Publication Data.
A catalogue record for this book is available from the British Library.

ISBN 978 0 7524 4732 2

Typesetting and origination by The History Press
Printed in Great Britain

CONTENTS

… the M25 is more than a road … it *means*. Our walk made something happen, happen to us. Nothing changed out there, in the drift of the motorists and their suspended lives; in my conceit, we were transformed. On a molecular level. Very gradually, and with considerable reluctance (on their part), forgotten ancestors acknowledge our feeble interventions. We re-lived their histories and remade our own. The noise of the motorway changed from nuisance to a chorus of oracle whispers, prompts, mangled information. Which we had volunteered to transcribe and interpret.

From Iain Sinclair's *Edge of the Orison: in the Traces of John Clare's 'Journey out of Essex'*

INTRODUCTION

CHOOSING THE ROAD
LESS TRAVELLED

Akeman Street is usually identified as a 78 mile Roman road joining St Albans (Verulamium) and Cirencester (Corinium) via the Roman town of Alchester, although some have suggested that it was originally a later Iron Age route. It is not mentioned in the early Roman literary sources of Britannia (but then neither is any road) and it certainly does not appear in the Late Roman Itineraries as a routeway, in fact it is missed off some maps of Roman Britain in the current literature (e.g. Jones and Mattingley 1990). Akeman Street seems to have been named at some time during the post-Roman period, most likely because it was seen as heading towards Bath where sick individuals (*aker* in Anglo-Saxon) could get cured of ailments in the hot water springs and so would travel along Acemannesceatre. There has been some ambiguity about the name as Thomas Codrington, the author of the first academic study of Roman roads of Britannia, related, 'It may be noticed that the name Iknild Street is sometimes given to Akeman Street on the east of Cirencester and that the Foss [Way] to the south-west of Cirencester is sometimes called Akeman Street'. However, there is also a contemporary route with the same name in Cambridgeshire.

The Roman Akeman Street has a strange symmetry. From Hemel Hempstead, where its route is first certain, it becomes the A4251, which as it travels west becomes the tortured A41 and, having cut through the Chiltern scarp, connects Tring with Aylesbury. Akeman Street moves stately through the Vale of Aylesbury still as the A41 and seems content to continue in its north-west direction into the West Midlands when, most un-Roman like, the isolated and iconic Arncott Hill uses its gravity to sling the road to a south-westerly course strangely bypassing the important Roman military base at Alchester. Akeman Street immediately recovers its surveyed poise and appears straight again, leading to a ford at Tackley. From the crossing of the Cherwell it becomes more elusive, its course hinted at by the lines of hedges and woods, some now grubbed out and only existing on old maps. Occasionally the road 'surfaces' as a straight track and a terrace obliquely moving down a sharp slope to cross a river, as at Stonesfield for the River Evenlode. At some points on its route to the Windrush valley it takes on the guise of lane again, but it is forgotten in high, wind-blown plateau of this atypical part of the Cotswolds, only becoming visible again as it terraces the valleys of the Coln and Leach. It is hidden almost completely until it reaches Cirencester, which it does in a most furtive fashion, enough to have it described as a later, subsidiary road of limited use. As far as I can ascertain from the literature associated with Roman roads or the journeys of travellers such as Defoe and Johnson, Akeman Street lacks the celebrity status of the Fosse Way or Watling Street and even the Sarn Helen in Wales, and I have probably been the first person to walk its whole length for a very long time.

This time-layered journey was prompted by my *Iron Age and Roman Wychwood: the Land of Satavacus and Bellicia* (2002), which was the result of walks within a 10 mile radius of my then home, the once market town of Charlbury in the Oxfordshire Uplands, more usually known for tourist consumption as the Oxfordshire Cotswolds. My archaeological prospecting was bounded by my 'day's walk' circle into an area that contains a whole range of tangible monuments and sites, including a possible later Iron Age *oppidum*, the North Oxfordshire Grim's Ditch, and the associated boundary of two tribes, the Catuvellauni to the east and the Dobunni to the west. There is also evidence for a Roman military presence, in the then newly discovered Roman military establishment at Alchester dated to AD 44. The area also contained a large number of villa and non-villa settlements, some of them surprisingly early. The Roman road known as Akeman Street traversed the landscape as a chord to my circle, so a study of its whole route was the logical way forward for an investigation of what had interested me most about the Wychwood area: its transition from the later Iron Age to the early Roman period. My focus had been considerably sharpened by a number of papers in *Britons and Romans: advancing an archaeological agenda* (James and Millett 2001). In one paper Barry Burnham and others explored the possible development of themes for urban research from *c.*100 BC to *c.*AD 200 where it was noted that there had been few studies directed at a wider analysis of settlement networks right across the periods responsible for determining settlement location, continuity and change. It was recognised that before such an analysis of the early Roman period could be undertaken it was necessary to re-evaluate the situation in the later Iron Age to hone our understanding of the development of Roman urbanism and whether or not it was a disruptive process or a comparatively smooth evolution from pre-conquest forms, with the early presence of the military helping or hindering the transformation. In another paper, Jeremy Taylor demonstrated the need for research in the area of rural society in the later Iron Age and its continuity or change into the early Roman period. Significantly, he commented on the lack of attention paid to the wider archaeological significance of roads and trackways that were incorporated within the conceptual world of peoples in the past as an extremely valuable resource in understanding how inter-communal social relations were mediated in the Roman countryside. These challenges prompted the issues that underlie the chapters of this book.

There was another side to the research that went into *Iron Age and Roman Wychwood*, that of the personal experience of movement through the landscape. I have always found walking a way of engaging and interacting with the world, providing a means of exposing myself to new, changing perceptions and experiences, and of acquiring a more intense awareness of my surroundings. Early on in my fieldwork it seemed that I was undertaking two modes of walking. The first was when I deliberately chose to use the jigsaw of paths and winding tracks that had resulted from the locally constituted boundaries of social and family networks (some originating possibly as far back as at least the later Iron Age) and their past space and which had been bound together through patterns of movement and mobility. When I walked the footpathed course of Akeman Street my perceptions were totally changed. I became acutely aware that the route that was knifing through my study area had a hypnotic 'onwardness', the past behind me and my linear future stretching out in front of me. There didn't seem to be a present. There was nothing 'local' about this intrusion as the straight, surveyed road seemingly disturbed the landscape through its determined assertiveness and authoritative understanding of the land, causing 'eddies' in the landscape which became villages and small towns in the Roman period. However, there was another facet of travelling the Roman Akeman Street: it told me exactly where to go and this in some way actually made me feel safe and secure. Somebody from the past was responsible for my actions; it was easy not to make decisions as they had already been made for me.

It was when I used Akeman Street's economy of time to get to an area of idiosyncratically shaped fields and footpaths where I could move more slowly through a surprising, and surprised landscape, that I realised that rather than the Roman road being surveyed to get from one *region* to another and the circuitous paths being a matter of moving from one *locality* to another within a region, the patterns of movement were in fact symbiotic. Akeman Street did not just pass through the landscape on its way to somewhere else, it was fed by an older landscape and reciprocally, it fed that landscape. Akeman Street was not just the action of an absent agent but its continuance as part of the landscape was the result of agency and identity. It is this sense of agency and identity through mobility and movement that I want also to explore in this book, with mobility defined by the circulation of people and ideas, goods and capital (Laurence 2001). What is important about this focus is that it centred on travellers passing through, and settlers living in, the landscape.

Interestingly, Jay Griffiths in her *Wild: An Elemental Journey* suggested that the configuration of the roads in the landscape represented ways of thinking.

Roman roads sliced through time ignoring everything that went before them, neutering the past and representing historic deeds of the conquering Empire. This linear past (identifying it as male and rational) of the road is the opposite to a cyclical, female, past of the older interweaving tracks, untainted by linear history.

Up until very recently the influence of Ivan D. Margary has provided the pervasive method of studying Roman roads by determining their routes through the landscape, and many community groups throughout England and Wales still undertake this valuable task of locating and excavating the remaining traces of these routes and publishing their work in local journals. It is important to understand the motivations and techniques used by a fascinating cast of travellers who developed these approaches and this will be the focus of the first chapter. However, when attempting to 'humanise' (Witcher 1997) Roman roads a whole new range of approaches is necessary based on movement and mobility changing or confirming identities, and the second chapter tentatively attempts to develop these perspectives. Throughout it is important to understand that this is not a competing set of methods, but that they complement each other in understanding the later Iron Age and Roman landscape. The remaining sections of the book explore journeys through Akeman Street's landscapes at three different points of time: the later Iron Age, the early Roman period and the late first and second centuries. As a result of those archaeological itineraries it should be possible to offer some insights into the agendas outlined above. I have used the very perceptive term of 'later Iron Age' developed by Tom Moore to indicate the period AD 10-43/60. Following recent academic convention, when discussing later Iron Age St Albans I have used the name 'Verlamion' and for the Roman town 'Verulamium'. I have arranged the Bibliography rather idiosyncratically, but I hope to reflect the nature of the journeys described in this book. There are a minimum of references cited in the text so as to not affect the immediacy of the movement. The Bibliography contains those works but also the other sources that I have used so as to form a 'paper trail' for further reading. While the chapters in the book form a relative chronology, I have arranged the Bibliography by place so as to bring out the elements of continuity present throughout the landscape of sources.

To those who travelled on Akeman Street before me, and whose studies I have used as vehicles for this book, I give my thanks. I am especially grateful to those county archaeologists along my route, Gloucestershire, Oxfordshire, Buckinghamshire and Hertfordshire, who gave me their help. Tom Moore let me see his dissertation and, along with Simon James, other materials before publication. My own work on the area of the North Oxfordshire Grim's Ditch has been significantly extended by Richard Massey in an unpublished MA dissertation and I am hugely grateful to him for giving me access to it. Tim Edensor provided sources and encouragement to engage with acts of walking and movement. The book is permeated by the approach of Richard Laurence, especially his *Roman Roads of Italy*, as well as Witcher's 1997 paper 'Roman Roads: phenomenological perspectives on roads in the landscape' and their ideas have become so embedded in my thinking that it is difficult to identify exactly where they are layered into the stratigraphy of the book. I hope they will take this as a compliment. Similarly, I was rescued at a very low period by Peter Fowler's 'Moving through the landscape' in the 1998 festschrift for Christopher Taylor. If I have taken a wrong turn, then it is my fault and not the directions people gave to me. A long-hidden epilepsy presented itself at the beginning of the research for this book and stopped me from driving. Lorna Scott was always willing to transport me to examine straight hedges and pottery-strewn fields, and was invaluable in the last stages of preparing the text for publication. Caro McIntosh prepared the illustrations and Grace Pritchard-Woods provided critical comments. As always, Boo provided encouragement and caring.

My interest in the past was nurtured by Gladys Mahoney, my aunt, who in my childhood took me to numerous museums and historic sites. It is to her, very belatedly, but with much love and respect, that I dedicate this book.

1

THERE AND BACK AGAIN

Underlying many studies of later prehistoric tracks there is almost a legendary quality that has many similarities with the maps on the endpapers of Tolkein's *Lord of the Rings*. Alfred Watkins' *Old Straight Track* may be an attractive, indeed seductive and mythical approach to identifying and explaining these routes in the context of 'ley lines' and the influence of elemental forces in the landscapes, water, rock and Celtic deities on their purposes and directions. Regrettably, the routes are the product of a very fertile mind – the author was a scholar, miller, archaeologist, naturalist, inventor, magistrate, county councillor, politician and leader of public opinion (Shoesmith 1990). There is often a consensus that although we know such tracks existed, it is often difficult to see their routes, or that it is simply impossible to find definitive proof of their roles in the landscape. Linear tracks such as the many 'ridgeways' or even specific routes such as the Icknield Way or the Jurrasic Way, which shadow or cut the route of Akeman Street, have been mainly proposed on the basis of physical geography and geology and 'restored' woodland (Harrison 2003). The most often-cited rationale for these long- and short-distance routes is that the valleys were full of dense woodland and so the long-distance tracks had to keep to the crests of hills, chalk or limestone if possible, where tree cover was either absent or less thick. The work of Christopher Taylor (1979) demonstrated that the monuments along these ridges – barrows and hillforts for example – were just a small sample of the density of sites in any area, the upstanding sites on the high ground being the results of differential survival – uplands-pasture-survival of monuments, valleys-arable-destruction of monuments – now retrieved through aerial photography. No doubt there were long-distance paths in the later Iron Age, but as Taylor so empathetically suggests, they were unlikely to have been only on 'ridgeways'. We should see the people of that period in a more kindly light as sophisticated, more involved in the day-to-day practicalities of farming and trading than in laying out mysterious lines of communication across the dark country and using them to carry out 'deeds of light'.

Andrew Sherratt's timely paper also brought pre-Roman routes into the wider perspective of long-distance trade, and identified the importance of water and rivers valleys in movement, considering that, although there had to be local routes along the scarp slopes of uplands on which hillforts were constructed, the long-distance routes were more likely to be medieval cattle drove roads keeping out of the populated and claimed land of the valleys (Sherratt 1996).

A similar, though less romantic, trajectory of ideas can be seen in the study of Roman roads. Thomas Codrington (1829-1918) was the first to analyse the origins of the names of the routes, the techniques of survey and engineering, and the history of the roads since post-Roman times. He was an engineer in late Victorian Britain and had a career background as an inspector for local government, during which time he published several works. His first publication was a report on the destruction of town refuse, published by Her Majesty's Stationery Office in 1888. This was only a pamphlet of 48 pages, including illustrations of furnaces in use at the time. He then went on to write the slightly more substantial 172 page work concerning the *Maintenance of Macadamised Roads* in 1879. However, his most authoritative work was *Roman Roads in Britain* (1905) which has influenced every subsequent study in this genre including, importantly, those of Ivan Margary. He identified the major Roman routes, and although Ivan Margary suggests that Codrington used a horse gig, there is never a feeling that he actually chose to travel Akeman Street, his main sources of information in defining its course being Ordnance Survey maps and county histories and journals.

Without doubt the doyen of the study of British Roman roads and their routes was Ivan D. Margary, who claimed that Thomas Codrington's work could not be improved, but only added to. Wounded in action at Gallipoli, he inherited a substantial sum of money which allowed him to spend much of his time tracing Roman roads. Margary's *Roman Roads in Britain*, 'a descriptive survey of the state of Roman roads – a surface description' (1955, 25), still remains the standard reference book and, through his allocation of a numbering system to the roads' courses, has underpinned every study since. This system was hierarchical with its starting point in Dover, the major Channel port used by the Romans. Single figures were used for main roads, 1 being Watling Street, the route of the AD 43 Invasion, double figures for secondary roads branching off main routes. Thus Akeman Street was designated 16a from St Albans to Alchester, because it was the sixth road to branch off Watling Street going north, and 16b from Alchester to Cirencester (*1*). Three figure references were used for minor roads, such as that diverging from Akeman Street at Stonehill to travel to Fleet Marston which was given the designation 162, i.e. the second subsidiary road leaving Akeman Street after its beginning at St Albans. His methods, and therefore an indication of his priorities, were detailed on several occasions (1955, 1962):

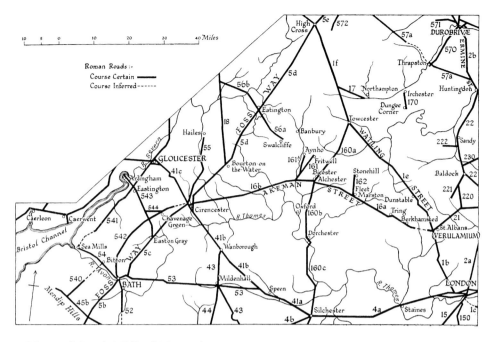

1 Margary's South Midland Network

1 Indoor preparation. Use the literature to find 'scraps of earlier information'. Study of place names, Ordnance Survey maps of increasing scales, and aerial photographs.
2 Fieldwork. Three stages: general reconnaissance, detailed examination of the whole route, and excavation of sections at a few selected points. 'It is the cumulative evidence of such traces [of roads] along a definite alignment that is the important feature'.
3 Publication in the local journal.

Margary's personal wealth enabled him to visit the routes of the Roman roads in a car at a time when cars were becoming more numerous. Although his attention to detail appears at first to belong to a pedantic man, his sense of humour is clearly apparent in his advice to motorised Roman road hunters: 'But the modern road is no fit place for meditation on antiquities and care is necessary if one wishes to pause and look about ... You have been warned!' (1962, 28). Margary did not see the point in walking whole stretches of road, 'a task which, though interesting, would hardly be justified in time and effort', though that he did walk short sections of Akeman Street is seen in his attention to the landscape: 'At Waddeson, beyond the park, the line is followed for a short distance by a back lane parallel to the village street and then by a footpath, where, just beyond a little pond by the school house, a piece of *agger* can be seen under a grove of yews'. He also notes a section of the road being indicated by a 'fine avenue of limes' (1955, 143).

In a review of the literature about Roman roads he demonstrated his values explicitly by berating previous studies and giving the top marks of 'excellent' to reports that were well surveyed, well illustrated with excellent observational details, beautifully produced folio volumes of maps, or showed consideration of the orientation and alignment of roads.

> Roman roads were consciously planned as a network of direct routes from centre to centre, like our railways, and the surveying for their construction was clearly the work of highly skilled engineers with a consummate grasp of the factors involved in choosing the best route. (1962, 92)

Perhaps it is the reference to railways that 'from centre to centre' implies that the length of disembodied linear space in between was important only as a structure for transport, with the main function of a train being speed rather than the scenery outside the window. The 'centre' seemingly sprang into life spontaneously and quite separately from the roads. The parallels with railways are stark. The *agger* of the Roman road roads is similar to the 'permanent way', the raised bed of chippings, insulated from the countryside by parallel ditches with a fence outside them, the trains not stopping between major cities. The 'up-line' and 'down-line' directions from London were very similar to Margary's own numbering system and he made a, now nostalgic, comparison of major Roman routes to the pre-Nationalisation railway routes.

Secondly, it is worth noting that with the 'descriptive' attributes of the most efficient route began a tradition of 'technist' views of Roman roads. Indeed, Margary left 40yds of the London to Lewes Way that he excavated to be preserved in perpetuity so that it might be visible to the public. He was a humble man and readily admitted that his survey was of the

> existing state of our knowledge of the roads, and in general no attempts have been made to fill in the gaps at missing portions or to discover new lines of road. Such work needs far more detailed investigation than can properly be done by a passing observer and is clearly a task for the archaeologist resident in the district. (1962, 25)

This task was taken up by the Viatores ('the travellers on Roman road') who were a group of 'amateur field workers' who met for six years under the chairmanship of Mr I.D. Margary, 'the leading authority of Roman roads in this country' to write *Roman Roads in the South-East Midlands*, which included Akeman Street. In front of me is a photograph of the 'Viatores in session' in 1957 with, unsurprisingly, a magisterial Margary at the head of the table looking with a shy smile straight into the camera. The table is occupied by seven other people who are also looking at the camera, though these are posed either with a finger on a scaled drawing or studying maps, working with a compass and straight ruler. Just as Margary enlisted the famous archaeologist O.G.S. Crawford, founder of the Ordnance Survey's

Archaeological Department and originator of the first Map of Roman Britain, to validate his book ('to assure the reader that the book is a serious and important contribution to knowledge and that the author can speak with authority') so Margary validates the Viatores' book: 'The purpose of this Foreword is just to assure its readers that the book is an important contribution ...'. There was a lot of insecurity in the students of Roman roads at this time, mainly because 'hunting' Roman roads was very much an amateur pursuit.

Around the table was R.W. Bagshawe, a younger fieldworker who was clearly much in awe of Margary as he details in his own book,

> an amusing etiquette developed between him [Margary] and his correspondents. If you believed you had discovered an unknown Roman road, you carefully collected all the facts and photographs and submitted them to him, the word 'Roman' being omitted if possible, 'ancient' or 'old' being used instead. Then, if, you were lucky, he would say, 'Your route may be worthy of inclusion' and later, almost as an afterthought, he would give it the next appropriate number. This was not done lightly or before a personal visit to the sites where the best parts existed. So it was that a Margary number became the highest honour one's research could achieve, personal and unique (Bagshawe 1979, 23).

The output of the Viatores' studies were maps, itineraries and linear descriptive text with no attempt at analysis.

16A AKEMAN STREET
ST ALBANS (VERULAMIUM) TO FLEET MARSDEN
24 MILES

> From the lane to Bottom House (SP956102) the course is continued north-westwards for 300 yards as far as the south-eastern tip of a narrow spinney, by a field boundary, which, although at present marked only by a fence, is shown on the Tithe of Wigginton, of 1841, to have been marked formerly by a hedge. In the south eastern tip of the spinney the *agger* is clearly visible, 30ft wide and 3ft high and stone may be felt with a probe. (Viatores 1964, 41-2)

It is interesting that there is almost a military correctness about the organisation of these studies, with Margary being the Commanding Officer. The military connection was underlined by one reviewer, Olwen Brogan (a female commenting on a male pursuit), who described the Viatores as 'explorers' with Margary as their 'counsellor', who needed 'courage' to search for the Roman roads in the London agglomeration, and wrote that they were 'fighting a rearguard action' against urban sprawl. Part of the impulse for this reaction may well have been the 'democratisation' of archaeology in the late 1960s and early 70s when rapid redevelopment of towns had given birth to urban archaeology in a rescue context.

In the face of such significant threats many British archaeologists saw Roman roads as unproblematic, easy to find and when excavated found to be predictably constructed. Archaeologists appeared to lose interest in roads once they had left the gates of the Roman town or city. For the 'interested amateur' Roman roads were 'safe' and disembodied – there was no need to people them because there were no people in the empty countryside, except for in the villas and these too were often the focus for non-professional excavation.

There is a very simple temporality at work here, the appearance of a single archaeological feature from the Roman phase in the landscape, and there has been a tendancy to ignore the evidence for a whole series of monuments of the same date and perhaps relationship to the road or its predecessors. Clearly the road is being treated as an abstract entity, a form of 'land art' like that of Richard Long (2002) which could be numbered, listed, quantified, mapped, safe and satisfying. The route of the road is extracted from the landscape, is a measured space, excluded from its surroundings both materially and cognitively. Margary's approach was to *represent* Roman roads as an impersonal function *inscribed* in the landscape and therefore disembodied from it and travellers through it. Margary and his students sought to replicate the past actions of the surveyor and constructor of the road in the present, in that they are interested mainly with the physical structure of Roman roads and in that their research paradigm is concerned with discovering the methods and results of this wish to inscribe a route on the land. To be fair, Margary and the Viatores never claimed to be interested in the traveller or any other aspect of Roman roads. This is clearly seen in Margary's suggestion that *Our Roman Highways* by Forbes and Burmester (1904) was 'complementary' to his approach but 'dealt primarily with the traffic, travellers, vehicles, road construction and maintenance and said little about routes'.

The most recent addition to the corpus of Roman road studies is *Roman Roads in Britain* (Davies 2004). Davies was professionally concerned with modern roads, having spent nearly 30 years in the Transport Research Laboratory, and continued the tradition of the study of Roman roads being undertaken by individuals who have not been professionally concerned with archaeology as a career, but have great expertise in the technology of transport. He identifies a whole new set of problems for investigation besides the routes of Roman roads – the dates of the roads, how they were planned and surveyed, what sort of traffic used them, and whether this use changed over time during the Roman period. Davies is writing about 'the roads as artefacts, built to assist people to journey efficiently from one place to another'. There are a number of references to Akeman Street from the 'database' providing the average depth of the metalling, 15cm (out of the 10 previous explorations identified) and its average width, 18m. Akeman Street is seen as a 'territory holding road' during the early period of the conquest. Clearly, the methods of enquiry result in detailed fieldwork along the roads' courses, and diagrams, tables, plans, maps and graphs are the relevant method of communicating the results of this assiduous fieldwork for what is an effective technical manual discussing aspects such as average gradient, culverts and bridges.

Davies also recognises that roads have a close relationship to issues of ideology, power, and identity (although he chooses not to explore them) and one intimately involved in our social constructions of the world, in that roads provide symbolic evidence for the coherence and extent of Roman influence in terms of exercising physical dominance over local populations, especially through defining distances of roads. It is quite clear from Davies' approach that the aspects of engineering he discusses so effectively are complementary to seeing Roman roads as social space and affecting the landscape in terms of power, culture and identity. It is this latter approach, of seeing a Roman road such as Akeman Street as a social construct, that produces a completely different set of problems, questions, methods and outcomes.

2

FROM SURVEYOR
TO TRAVELLER

The maps of Akeman Street, road 16a and b, constructed by Margary and his colleagues, locate the viewer outside the scene being depicted and therefore produce a highly sectional view of the past with all its archaeological connotations. It might be thought that there are advantages to using abstract space so that traces of the road can be located in its totality, however such maps create an entity which is 'independent of any point of observation [that could only be] directly apprehended by a consciousness capable of being everywhere at once and nowhere in particular' (Ingold 1993, 155). Such two-dimensional representations record the *inscription* of the route of the road but are independent, and as such this denies any sense of the process of movement through the landscape. These route maps, valuable as the beginnings of landscape explorations, present a view that would have been completely incomprehensible to those who lived alongside and travelled the road in the Iron Age and Roman periods. The road is also presented as linear, allowing only forward and return journeys, and is easily measured in terms of Roman miles, marching distance per day, and average distance between roadside settlements – all valuable information and making absolute sense to a life lived on a flat plane.

However, in contrast, if Roman roads are considered to be *embodied* in the landscape a *movement* of change and continuity, causation and outcome results. This embodiment in the landscape is the result of roads seen not as being built through abstract space, but through cultural spaces produced by people, and their mobility within them (Witcher 1997). Clearly, identifying this incorporation/ embodiment will be much more difficult than locating a predetermined line which joins two or more settlements across a region; rather it will show how settlements along the route are related to the road and vice versa. This chapter is an exploration of how this might be achieved and, clearly, in setting up a perspective

across long distances. Even though we can't usually identify the individuals and groups who build roads, we can offer interpretations of their motivations and the resulting function of the routes, and by doing so get a little closer to those people and their modifications of the landscape.

MOVEMENT AS PATTERNS IN THE LANDSCAPE

The complexity of the landscape on the ground seems to be held together by linear archaeological features and this 'held togetherness' is the result of movement and mobility by individuals and communities, and these patterns have been described as 'place ballets' (Seamon 1995). The giving of form to the experience of movement is the building of roads and other structures which become fixed into the landscape. Tim Ingold (2000) has produced a framework that allows us to put Akeman Street into the landscape as a linear pattern which holds together, and is held together by, that landscape. He would see the landscape of later Iron Age and early Roman Akeman Street as a world that was known to those who dwelt in it and who inhabited its places and journeyed along roads, reflecting landscape, movement and identities. While Ingold has identified 'dwellers' as the inhabitants of the landscape, for the purposes of this study it will be necessary to divide that definition into two symbiotic sub-sets: 'settlers' and 'travellers'. The overlapping set can be where settlers and travellers share repertoires of mobility and movement. So, already we have the possibility of seeing 'travellers' along Akeman Street who can undertake journeys of short and long distances, and 'settlers' who also can live along and alongside the road, or as far each side of it as the road has an influence. In some ways individuals might be both, or one might change into the other depending on the 'identity routes' that have been experienced.

The relationship of the terms 'settler' and 'traveller' is defined by how different or complementary the activities that they carry out is. Both the sedentary and mobile activities along the route of Akeman Street would be called a 'taskscape' by Ingold. He further describes the 'landscape' as the 'congealed taskscape' – it is made up of many 'collapsed' activities that are detectable and provide us with the archaeological evidence that we need to construct the tasks that the settlers and travellers undertook. Akeman Street is one of those congealed taskscapes which can be studied either quantitatively as a three-dimensional engineered entity with length, width and depth (as Margary did), or qualitatively by looking for evidence of the experience of movement, mobility and identity in relation to collapsed activities through which it runs and on either side of the road.

What sort of tasks might have collapsed and how could we attach meaning to them and develop an insight into their relation to individual and group identities? The tasks of settlers encompass manufacture, economic activities, agriculture requiring products and ideas, production of materials for market, and looking after travellers – more complex evidence of power and memory etc. which was manifested in towns, villas, village tracks and long stretches of earthworks. Identifying the activities and interactions that formed and reformed identities and that were undertaken by the travellers is more difficult, as evidence for the movement perspective will be much harder to find since it is ephemeral and leaves much less trace than the evidence for settlement. The retrieval of artefacts indicates trading, but it is difficult to pin down which specific routes were used. The development of the monumentality of towns and the architecture of villas are indications of the migration of culture and ideas, and perhaps they signify the importance of the arterial roads built by the Roman authorities for this purpose. Although an elegant way of looking at landscape, Ingold's scheme needs to have some relationship to an individual's perception of landscape and the inter-layering of tasks and movement that were undertaken by travellers and settlers through time.

MOVEMENT AS PERSONAL EXPERIENCE

Margary's and similar approaches produce interpretations of the road that are difficult to challenge and as there are no human interactions any number of journeys might take place. We need to think of roads in a psychological context as well as material and functional, and a methodology for developing a 'used' and 'felt' perspective for the traveller needs to be identified (Soja 1996). We need to think of *specific* journeys that are organised around the passage of a traveller, and their perimeters and parameters of sight or experience. As soon as a route is seen as identity-forming then movement and action become a corollary and roads and paths seem also to be used as metaphors for an outcome – a sign of action and agency of one or more entities. Through the action of movement, a road draws together aspects of places and the biography of spaces, or perhaps in the case of this book, places draw together aspects of the road and the biography of the road. The road also gives the opportunities and experiences that changes who 'we' are and creates personal and community histories. In each case both the road and the place, the individual and community will be intimately related to identity – an event and a place might not easily be separated, as they are often of the same essence – since they are constructed by individuals who have had experiences as settlers and travellers.

The psychological contexts of roads can be approached through the methodology of phenomenology which derives from the concept of space as a social product, an active and dynamic way of looking at locality as opposed to space being seen as merely a 'linear container'. As a social product the significance and importance of a locality can only be appreciated as part of a movement to and from it – in relation to others the act of moving may be as important as arriving (Tilley 1994, 31). So, phenomenology is an explicit attempt to provide us with a way of thinking through movement across landscape. Importantly, Tilley suggests that his research might be described as 'middle range' in so far as it is aimed at filling a gap between the site plan and the distribution map. Here the gap is seen as being filled by movement along a road.

I have chosen a phenomenological approach because it is related to movement through the metaphors of paths not bound to space but being the 'between' of 'to' and 'from' and being as close as we can get to the perspective of travellers, most of whom would not have travelled the whole road, and who would have used directions, terrain, settlements and specific iconic localities such as shrines as verbal cartographies (Riley *et al.* 2005). Phenomenological approaches are ways of respecting and making explicit experiences as well as maintaining a perspective of the social meanings of the past that these approaches might produce. The experience of movement from which this book is written has been on foot as I chose to walk the whole length of Akeman Street in order to be able to observe the route in a detail that could not be experienced through documents or maps or place names. I shared with Margary the ideal of detailed examination of the whole route, though I suspect in his case it was largely by car. In my case I have only used the phenomenological approach through walking experiences and since other modes of movement, such as bicycle/horse riding, driving or being driven, would share itineraries and paths of observation, they would produce different experiences and knowledge of the environment.

MOVEMENT THROUGH TIME

Margary's maps of the Roman road network create an entity which is timeless, with neither a date for the road nor for the tasks that were undertaken alongside it. However, a temporal context is needed to see changes in the road and the structures and landscapes around it and within it. These changes are a crucial dimension in the formation and reformation of identity at personal, group and community levels. Perhaps the hardest part of structuring an alternative way of understanding Roman roads and the people who used them is this temporality.

We have no mention of Akeman Street in any Roman itinerary to help us know that at least at a particular time it was in use. Neither the title of 'Akeman Street' nor Margary's number categories of '16a' and '16b' are contemporary with the road; in fact it is only presumed that the road was allocated the former name in the Anglo-Saxon period, or indeed that the explanation given in the Introduction for the name actually referred to this route. Trying to use the stratigraphy of the road is also fraught with difficulties as it is formed of several re-layerings and is extremely hard to interpret, as later traffic, especially at times of economic decline when the road was not resurfaced, will have worn it away. Up until recently sections through Roman roads, including those few across Akeman Street, were often interpreted by the excavators in schematic form and reflect what they

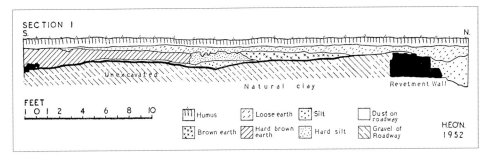

2 Section across Akeman Street at Quenington. *Source: Bristol and Gloucester Archaeological Society Transactions Vol 76, p. 36*

were looking for, informed by Classical literature or visits to high-status sites such as North Leigh or those on the Continent, rather than the remains they actually found (2). Another temporal problem is that one layer of metalling looks very much like another and consecutive layers of post-Roman re-surfacing are virtually indistinguishable from earlier ones, unless modern bricks or other broadly dateable materials are apparent in the make up of the layers, and then some sort of meaningful relative chronology can be recovered.

If the road is treated as an archaeological artefact it will be its association with structures alongside it that will be important in providing a stratigraphic relationship, but there are also problems with this approach. In the countryside ditches often separated the road from the upstanding edifices along its route, and these ditches were usually cleaned to provide more material for the road's surface, and therefore relationships with any structures are now hard to identify. In small towns where there probably weren't any ditches, because stopping animals from wandering onto the road was not an issue, it is still very difficult to match the stratigraphy of any structures aligned to the road to its re-metallings, especially when the roadside structure itself cannot be dated. Unfortunately, there is no typological sequence for Roman roads as their characteristics of straightness and similar construction were maintained over a long period, and in many cases are still in use today.

So, the writing of biographies of roads is not straightforward and can produce an over-simplistic and partial a view of time – safe and descriptive, less speculative and less interesting – and stops higher levels of interpretation and synthesis of experience in their tracks. Perhaps it is the experience of travellers in the countryside that might help in setting up some sort of temporality and give the road some sort of temporal profile. My own walking of the course of Akeman Street took in multiple temporalities, not only the present, but also those of all the monuments of different periods along the route (Lucas 2005, 41). It must have been the same for travellers in the past. The landscape that they were travelling through provided a present, but also they knew, or learnt about, the past practices in the landscape through the collapsed activities around them, some of which were significant as continuing locales of memory and power.

If we want to try to reconstruct the landscape that the traveller experienced we need to develop a temporality of the road through 'association' which would view the road as an integral part of the landscape, but also the landscape as being an integral part of the road, and not just in a chronological relationship to the structures alongside it (Aldred 2002; Petts 1998). This would put the onus onto constructing temporalities of landscape in order to have sequential 'taskscapes' which have 'congealed' over long periods of time – I call these 'timescapes'. My choice of dates to travel Akeman Street are dependent on these 'timescapes' – the later Iron Age, the Roman conquest period, the later first century to the early second century – because at each stage there were identifiable monuments, *oppida*, military establishments, the early villas and the beginning of the *civitas* capitals, and since change is harder to locate, the second and third centuries. However, we should not expect to see change at the same rate along its path, or a similar set of peoples living in the same way and having the same attitudes or identities. Hopefully, this will give an 'organic' temporality of growth and decay, and, as important, the curation of activities through the traveller's own temporality in the landscape will give a sense of how localities were seen to have continuity or change embedded in them, especially through features that told of identity and power. This produces 'deep maps' that acknowledge the way that memory and associative landscape are layered and interleaved. In this way, although we cannot know the names and personalities of the travellers, perhaps we can begin to understand their experiences and have a limited dialogue with them.

ARCHAEOLOGICAL APPROACHES TO THE LANDSCAPE OF AKEMAN STREET

There have been a number of influential studies on the biographies of Roman roads by Laurence (1998, 1999 and 2001) using documentary evidence of the people and personalities of Roman Italy, as well as the structures and processes of the archaeologist, to interpret the role and functions of roads. The reverse is the case with Roman roads in Britain, because there are no accounts of travel. We have to rely on the archaeology to help us identify the material aspects of the road and approaches such as phenomenology to consider the experience of the traveller.

It is one thing to discuss the theoretical underpinnings of a different approach to moving through landscapes, but how can this be related to the physical evidence of the ground, the 'taskscapes'? How can the processes of making the landscape, representing identities and naming them in the past, be perceived, interpreted, reused and decoded in the present? Johnson has suggested an agenda for an archaeology of historic landscapes, which can be adapted to emphasise movement and mobility (2007, 149-52). While it might be argued that Akeman Street is in a 'proto-historic' landscape, there is so little epigraphy along its route and no direct documentary evidence that in reality it is partially in a 'prehistoric' landscape. Johnson argues that archaeological sources have an integrity that equals that of documents where many aspects of everyday life are not recorded formally, and this is illustrated in the case of Akeman Street – we are likely to be able to identify a peasant in a deserted medieval village such as Tapwell, 2km north-west of North Leigh villa, or the village's population in a particular year, whereas we know nothing about the owner of the nearby Roman complex, one of the most palatial in the later province and clearly the residence of some highly important individual. However, the archaeology of North Leigh can give us a sense of upper-class life and daily life in the Roman period. Johnson's agenda can be modified to meet the needs of this study:

i) The use of individual landscapes and not generalisations, putting aside the idea of the 'Roman road' as artefact and focusing on the route through which it travels.

ii) The encouragement of a contextual account of everyday realities of social life in the landscape, using the phenomenological approaches to movement and mobility and the effects that they have on identity formation.

iii) Arranging the discussion around the very basic parameters of space and time:
   a) Examining chosen localities along Akeman Street to identify smaller/ larger agricultural settlements, ritual settlements, movements within the village/villa etc.
   b) Exploring patterns of movement across the landscape and their everyday realities, and at different scales of temporality, from within a day's walk to seasonal constraints; changes across decades.

iv) Discovering and exploring locales of power and memory in the landscape, examining sites such as *oppida* and towns, the relationships of movement to them and inside them and comparison with previous and future temporalities.

v) Having reached an understanding of a place along the route of the road at a particular point in time, we might consider archaeologies of changes that were brought to this pattern of life at various critical junctures and how this compares to activity along the whole road. In terms of this study the dates would be set broadly as we have no means of producing an overall historical, or archaeological, chronology based on documentary or absolute dates from archaeological evidence so broad – 'timescapes' will be used: the later Iron Age (*c.*AD 10-60) and the early Roman period (*c.*AD 43-200).

vi) The study could then move outwards conceptually, while still focusing on the landscape of Akeman Street, to wider issues concerned with settlement location, continuity and change in rural and urban contexts and the development of new identities.

vii) Finally, the outcomes could be developed into the wider archaeological significance of roads and trackways, and be useful in showing how the issues and processes identified on Akeman Street might be replicated/different from those on other routes, and further, what this can tell us about life across the later Iron Age/early Roman period and how the one interfaces or overlaps with the other.

It is hoped that using the theoretical background developed in this chapter will implicitly give new insights not just into the road as an artefact, but a route through populated landscapes and the complexities that accompany that assumption.

3

LATER IRON AGE
AKEMAN STREET?

It has been suggested that Akeman Street, perhaps more than for any other Roman road, was preceded by a later Iron Age or earlier route, later being given the 'full treatment' by being straightened and surfaced (Johnson 1979). It is the presence of *oppida* at the beginning and end of the Roman Akeman Street, Verlamion and Bagendon, that has led to the supposition that there must have been a route *between* them, and that therefore Roman Akeman Street must have a precursor. This interpretation is further strengthened by the Roman road linking Verulamium and Corinium as *civitas* capitals. As with all pre-Roman routes there are difficulties in demonstrating that such a course existed, especially as, unlike Roman routes, they were not surveyed and in many cases may have been braided with different streams of traffic, cattle or traders using lines at different times of year, and the whole course migrating back and forth across the landscape over decades if not centuries, and well into and throughout the Roman period. Chance finds of high-status sophisticated goods might suggest trading along a specific route, but items such as brooches, coins and precious metals don't often drop off the back of wheeled vehicles or out of sacks carried by horses, and are more likely to be the result of deposition for some specific reason rather than casual loss. Perhaps a better indicator of movement and mobility would be settlement evidence. Unfortunately, settlement evidence is not easy to come by when soils do not show up traces of ephemeral structures from the air, and most later Iron Age pottery ploughed to the surface breaks down when the water in its voids freezes in winter. What do survive are the earthworks of large settlements known as *oppida*. These have attracted attention for several hundred years and have been investigated in greater depth than other aspects of the later Iron Age landscape. They represent probably the most important evidence in terms of understanding the routes and significance of long-distance trails.

VERLAMION

This first journey begins in the second quarter of the first century AD above what is now St Albans (*3*).

Travellers on their way west from Camulodunum would have crested the low hill east of Verlamion, at a point determined by Beech Bottom Dyke which they had had to follow across the plateau behind them. Their attention would have been caught immediately by the changing of the thickness of the track from a wide, braided entity into a narrow, single route. The traveller would have no problems in identifying the significance and function of the square central enclosure in the valley bottom as it was next to a marshy area through which ran the River Ver. Here rituals were carried out by powerful people who struck the coins that travellers had seen or heard about and were gifts to other important people who led smaller, less important communities than the one below. This central enclosure was certainly important as it was accentuated by the two sides of the Fosse earthwork, defining a space around it and re-emphasising its square shape and importance. The travellers' gaze would have been drawn also to a structure that dominated the skyline opposite, its roof being visible above high earth banks and with an impressive wooden gateway. This was the long-lived and chameleon-like site of Gorhambury; its importance would have been accentuated by the path connecting it with the central enclosure (Neal *et al.* 1984). The travellers might have wondered if the person whose face was on the coins was in the enclosure, or the structure on the break of the valley slope. Also on the opposite side of the valley but separated from Gorhambury by a very shallow dry valley was another set of earthworks, now in Prae Wood, that were not so impressive and had no access to the valley through a gate or causeway. The banks appeared to control movement behind them, especially cattle and sheep, stopping them straying into the valley. The very narrow tracks that moved in a north to south direction along the valley bottom were diverted obliquely up the slope, to disappear behind the earthworks. From the crest of the eastern slope of the valley on which the traveller stood, only tops of the roofs and upper parts of some of the wooden structures showed above the Prae Wood earthworks, some being higher and better built than others, and the traveller could guess that these were probably the focus of a family or community group less important than those who lived at Gorhambury. As they moved down the gentle slope of the valley their route was deliberately set to pass a shrine, with a bank in front of it, which was directly above and visible from the central enclosure. This location, at the present Folly Lane, was destined to become much more iconic in the near future. At the bottom of the valley, and after crossing the marshy area on a timber

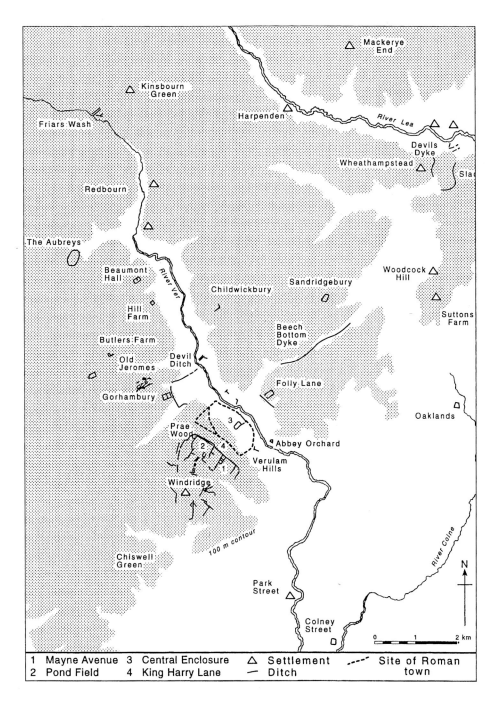

3 The Verulamium area in the late pre-Roman Iron Age. *Courtesy of Rosalind Niblett, drawing by Philip Dean*

causeway, the travellers would have found themselves in front of the central enclosure, but with its high banks denying a view inside indicating a very special area to which, at least to them, access was forbidden. The travellers' ongoing route across the valley bottom and up its western slope was determined by the White and New Dykes, ditches on the downhill side of the slope, which would have had the effect of both controlling their movements and, as they turned around to look back into the valley, re-emphasising the importance of the central enclosure. The Devil's Ditch controlled access into the valley from the north by being an extension of the Gorhambury enclosure. Ahead and above, the Gorhambury settlement could still be seen and clearly dominated the trade route and the valley, its buildings still visible above its earthworks. The roof lines of the Prae Wood farmstead were now hidden by the continuous dykes, giving the impression of being a natural extension of the hill slope and that the settlement behind them did not exist. The lack of ditches in front of the earthworks indicated that they must be on the uphill side and been kept clean to provided the spoil for the earthworks due to the ongoing need to retain the height of the dykes in the face of soil creep into the valley. In between the Fosse and the Prae Wood enclosure could be seen the burial place for the populace on the west side of the valley, the King Harry cemetery.

Reaching the crest of the west side of the valley and looking back, the central enclosure with its screen of the Fosse was still the most dominant feature in the valley landscape, and it was also clear that the whole settlement was on a south-west north-east axis, reflecting the direction of the trade route, but the trade route was still policed visually by the Gorhambury dykes now above and to the right. To the left the Prae Wood area was still not visible and could not be seen from the Gorhambury structures either. Looking back across to the opposite crest of the valley where the panorama had first opened out, the shrine could still be seen and its relationship with the central enclose re-enforced. Although the Gorhambury structure was obviously the most high-status structure on the hillside, it was in the Prae Wood settlement and outside on the western plateau that most of the trading and exchange took place.

It would have been quite strange to have left a valley with so much power within it to move on to the clay and flint plateau with its small settlement groups and embanked fields and drove ways. However, as the road moved west across the plateau any traveller from the opposite direction would have anticipated a landscape of power and ritual ahead from the presence of a small ritual site at Wood End Lane. Here traders and travellers would give thanks for protection on their long journey. Gorhambury on the eastern horizon would have been visually linked with this ritual site. As the travellers from the west reached the Gorhambury site it would be the central enclosure at the bottom of the valley which would have commanded their attention (4).

Most of this detail has been taken from Rosalind Niblett's excellent *Verulamium* (2001) as well as *Alban's Buried Towns* (Niblett and Thomson 2005), but the

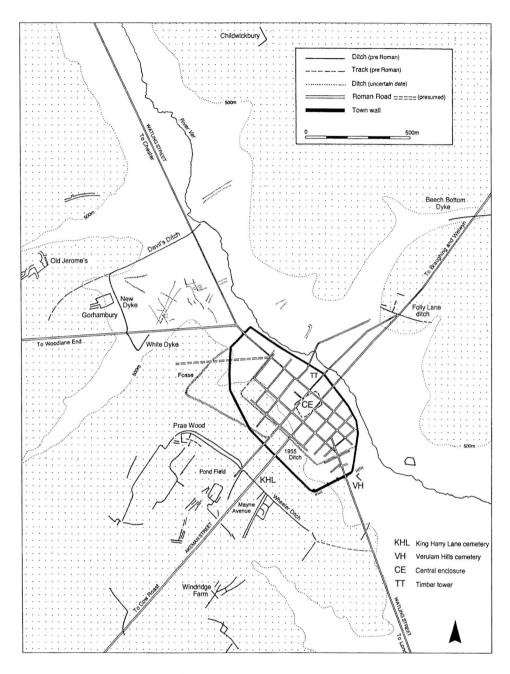

4 The Verulamium *oppidum* in the early first century AD. *Courtesy of Rosalind Niblett, drawing by David Williams*

interpretation is my own. The intention of the narrative was to demonstrate that in later Iron Age Verlamion the whole valley was seething with signs of power, ritual and control, each dependent on the others for effectiveness. While the archaeology is quite complex in its detail, it is very easy to forget that the patterns of evidence that we collect can sometimes 'lock' us into just one small locality, the single structure, and that we can lose the sense of life in the past that was largely a function of movement around a settlement (Hunn 1995).

Where the route of a later Iron Age Akeman Street enters the Verlamion complex is not known for certain, even assuming that there was one route and not several in a braided course. Other routes may have bypassed the settlement altogether as access might have been permitted only to individuals or groups of high status. The important issue for any traveller was that of understanding the messages given by the well-delineated areas, of the communal aspect of the valley as opposed to the private functions of the areas behind the dykes on its lip. Clearly, other later Iron Age and Roman sites along Akeman Street are not as well known or as accessible as the St Albans landscape and it would be foolish to try such a construction where there is limited evidence. However, the point to be emphasised is that we can propose lines of movement archaeologically and suggest how they give significance to, and are made significant by, areas of landscape and settlement (5).

ASHRIDGE/COW ROAST

Verlamion was in a good position to exploit newly opened Gallic markets, and the reason for its founding and subsequent success must have been consequent on elite groups exploiting the smelted iron ore from the Cow Roast valley site and Ashridge on the plateau above. This smelted iron ore was an important economic resource for the elites based at Verlamion who controlled the routes eastwards, so much so that the whole settlement pattern was based on the route from Cow Roast to Camulodunum. The Cow Roast site is 15km from Verlamion and 4km from the Tring Gap and sits in the bottom of the Bulbourne valley, which forms an important route through the Chiltern Hills (Morris and Wainwright 1995; Zeepvat 1997). The River Bulbourne, which rises as a spring at Northchurch, was significant in providing the water that was needed in the iron smelting process all along the valley. Cow Roast appears to have been a substantial centre with Bronze Age and later Iron Age coins, pottery and a number of burial sites, indicating that there was considerable activity in the area. Some indications from the Roman coinage distribution suggest that the site was already prosperous before AD 43 and therefore probably important in the preceding period. However, the later Roman villas in the valley and on the plateau have no known traces of later Iron Age structures below them, and it might be possible that any production was controlled directly from Verlamion (Neal 1999). Considering its position on a

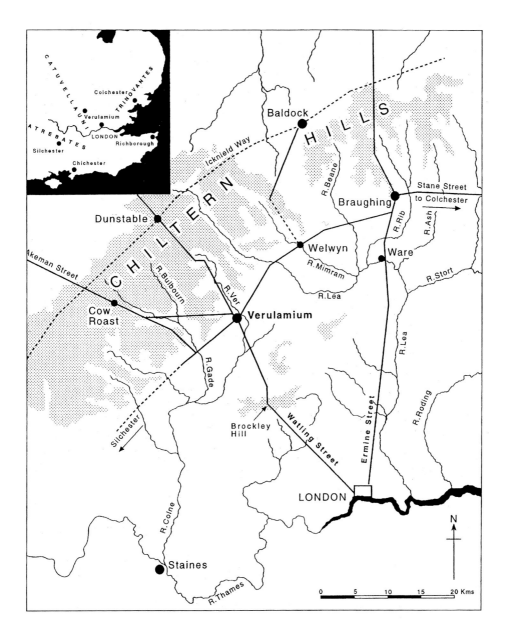

5 Verulamium in relation to major Roman roads and settlements in the area. *Courtesy of Rosalind Niblett, drawing by Philip Dean*

major route from Verlamion, the lack of imported pottery indicates a middle - to low-status settlement concerned also with agriculture. There is some evidence of pre-Roman iron smelting of 'bog' ore from the immediate vicinity, and possibly also evidence that it was transported from deposits in Northamptonshire. Four shaft furnaces for the production of iron bloom have been excavated as a group on an Iron Age site at Dellfield, Berkhampsted (Thompson and Holland 1976). These were situated at 152m above sea level on the northern slope of the Bulbourne valley overlooking Berkhampsted and facing west, which although in the direction of the prevailing wind, may have had something to do with the presence of structures close by to the west so that the fumes and smoke might be carried away in the opposite direction.

Above Cow Roast, on the clay and flint plateau of Ashridge, is a remarkable relict landscape, unploughed since the pre-medieval period, so that earthwork features have survived intact and in some cases quite 'crisp'. Extensive survey and fieldwork in an area have identified a large number of earthworks of various pre-medieval dates. At least three enclosures of later Iron Age date were joined to field systems and within these enclosures there appears to have been some sort of compartmental design indicating different, as yet unknown, functions (Bryant and Niblett 1997). These enclosures are part of a wider landscape with identifiable farmsteads, field boundaries and drove ways, evidenced by the large number of later Iron Age pottery sherds found, the total assemblage being larger than those of the Roman period. It is probable that the plateau was the source of the fuel which was a defining factor in the continuation of the industry in the valley below for 300 years and this indicates a well-managed natural resource. The configuration of human activity on the plateau might indicate what the area above Verlamion was like before heavy ploughing destroyed it.

BIERTON

The Tring Gap through the Chiltern scarp would be the perfect place for a settlement controlling trade, or at least acting as an exchange centre, and Bierton is just 3km from the breach in these hills. The site also lies just 2km from the route of later Akeman Street and the same distance from Aylesbury and it appears to be the first settlement of any pretension since Verlamion, some 30km to the east. This later Iron Age site covered several hectares, with a substantial 'Belgic' ditched enclosure, but was only in use for a comparatively short period, possibly the first half of the first century AD after which the enclosure ditch was deliberately filled with either bank material or organically rich rubbish rather than natural silting. Excavations in 1979 detected four phases of occupation, the earliest being connected with an 'open' or 'simple' enclosure which developed into a 'complex, ditched' settlement (Allen 1986). Significantly, large amounts of imported Gallo-Belgic and Central Gaulish pottery, particularly 'Terra Rubba' from the Tiberian-Claudian period were found and were likely to have come through the Bulbourne valley with the potin coin, as well as brooches from the Camulodunum area. What is interesting is that on domestic sites imported pedestal-shaped vessels of the period are usually rare compared to cups and platters. However, of the Bierton assemblage over three-quarters were pedestal cups, which might indicate an important 'down the line' trading link. Traces of ovens, cattle and sheep suggested a mixed farming economy and may have contributed to a market-centre role.

The amount of bog-ore in the Bulbourne valley is unlikely to have been enough for such a large industry over such a long period and that is why imports from Northamptonshire might have been necessary, and may well have given the Bierton settlement considerable political status. That there might have been quite a large well-distributed settlement area with a number of economic foci, and possibly an important social and perhaps political role, is indicated by a significant amount of later Iron Age pottery and evidence for a hillfort in Aylesbury which has been produced (Farley and White 1981). While it may be attractive to consider that the Roman Akeman Street was following a later Iron Age route between Bierton and the Alchester area, the almost complete lack of identified settlement for this period in the Vale of Aylesbury might point to the opposite conclusion. While Bierton was no doubt related to the Cow Roast sites perhaps the main axis of movement of goods was below the Chiltern scarp and south to Maidenhead and the Thames, and that trade route was the origin of the pedestal cups.

AVES DITCH

The fact that a Roman fort(ress) was constructed by AD 44 gives the Alchester area a special significance in the later Iron Age. Why was it important to have a military establishment, seemingly unconnected with the early Roman course of Akeman Street, in place at so early an opportunity? The later Iron Age archaeology of the area immediately around the fort(ress) site has thrown up little of significance except farmsteads, some banjo enclosures and a large number of late Iron Age coins all of which would be unlikely on their own to explain why such a determined early response by the Roman government occurred. North of the later route of Akeman Street no enclosure sites are to be found within 3km, and south of the route 6km, indicating that it was built through an area lacking in earlier settlement (6).

The most impressive evidence for the existence of possible later Iron Age activity in the area is Aves Ditch (or Wattle Bank), an enigmatic, virtually straight linear monument 4.2km long. The date and function of Aves Ditch have been variously considered to be a pre-Roman tribal boundary, a Roman road or an Anglo-Saxon boundary. In the 1997 excavations the earliest feature in the three trenches (one of which did not completely section the bank) was a curving ditch, dated to the mid

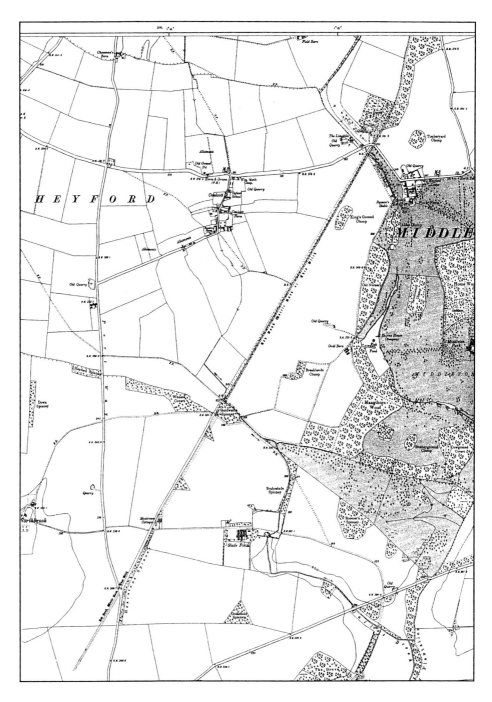

6 Extract of the 1:10560 Ordnance Survey map, Oxfordshire sheet XXII of 1923 showing straight, southern section of Aves Ditch earthwork reduced to 1:20,000 (after Sauer 2005)

to late Iron Age, and certainly cut by Aves Ditch and therefore earlier. It is highly likely that this was a banjo enclosure – the amount of mid Iron Age pottery and bone from possible feasting does point to this conclusion. Evidence from the ditch of the enclosure indicated that it was constructed in a cleared landscape and that it began to silt-up between 500 and 325 BC. Aerial photographs show a number of other sub-circular enclosures on both sides of Aves Ditch which have not been dated by excavation, but could be the source of residual pottery in the bank. The first edition of the one-inch Ordnance Survey of England and Wales Sheet 61 Banbury (Buckingham) indicates that there is an extension of the straight section increasingly curving north-west, perhaps in a discontinuous fashion, as far as Souldern with an offset gap at Chilgrove. However, selected excavation along the proposed line of this extension has demonstrated that it is more likely to be the result of the construction of Roman and medieval roads.

The most recent excavations indicated that the straight section of the Aves Ditch was of the late Iron Age. This was on the basis of three narrow trenches, one of which could not be extended to the rear of the earthwork (Sauer 2005a). Sixty years previously three sections cut across a linear feature's course to the south-west had suggested a Roman origin for Aves Ditch. As a seeming compromise the excavator suggested that the monument was constructed in the later Iron Age as a tribal boundary by aristocratic elites who had considerable contacts with the Roman Empire. Considering that there is so little later Iron Age occupation to the east of this linear monument such an interpretation poses considerable problems and what must be considered in more depth is the relationship of the wider landscape and other archaeological features within that landscape to Aves Ditch.

Aves Ditch appears to delimit an area of gentle west–east tilted plateau above the steep valley sides of the Cherwell. At no point is the earthwork inter-visible with the edge of the Cherwell valley. That it cannot be seen from the valley floor of the Cherwell indicates that there did not need to be a defensive or otherwise inter-visual link between them. Aerial photography has demonstrated that the plateau west of the line of Aves Ditch had a fairly even distribution of settlement in the form of six banjo enclosures and several curvilinear and rectangular features which are situated alongside the routeways (Featherstone and Bewley 2000). This density of later Iron Age settlement was greater than that to the east of Aves Ditch.

Inside the plateau area defined by the edge of the Cherwell valley scarp and Aves Ditch there appear to be two important routes. One, the Portway, comes from the direction of Kings Sutton (where there is known to be a later Roman settlement but as yet only a small amount of Iron Age material) and negotiates the scarp slope obliquely. The route almost bisects the plateau area north–south before cutting the Aves Ditch near Kirtlington Park. It then appears to traverse the slope to cross the Cherwell at Enslow. The direction of travel would be pronouncedly north–south, with any later Iron Age route on the later course of Akeman Street being a track into the North Oxfordshire Grim's Ditch area.

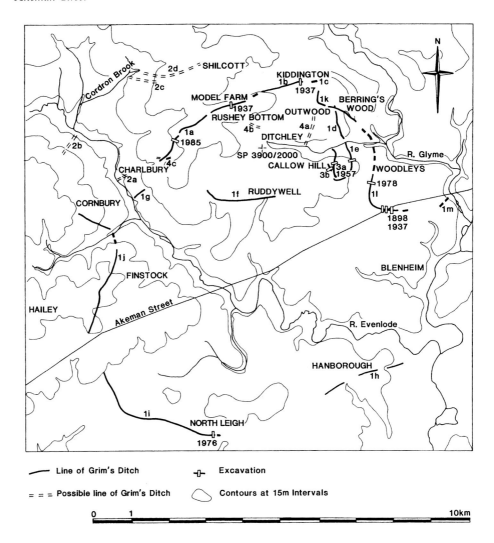

7 The North Oxfordshire Grim's Ditch Phases One and Two

sides. The source of the valley is a spring, producing a very marshy area and the resulting stream then flows through further boggy deposits, the Devils Pool/ Ditchley Bottom, through the Phase One earthworks before its meeting with the River Glyme.

Massey has presented some highly significant insights into the function of the Phase One area through a study of the rich aerial photograph cover completed in 1995 when due to a variety of circumstances (the weather and the ability to use the airspace freed by the decommissioning of the USAF base at Lower Heyford) some magnificent, and at times eloquent and evocative, soil and crop-mark images recorded much of the ephemeral detail of the area. Massey's assiduous study of these aerial images, and his consequent fieldwork, have identified a dense distribution of

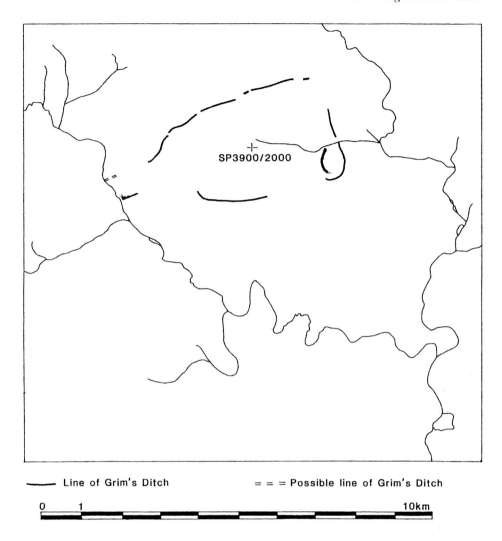

SP3900/2000

—— Line of Grim's Ditch   = = = Possible line of Grim's Ditch

0   1   10km

8 The North Oxfordshire Grim's Ditch Phase One

'*Viereckschanzen*', sometimes with internal and external rows of pits. This class of monument has a number of diagnostic features in that they have a tendency to be isolated from surrounding settlements, laid out geometrically as precise squares or near–squares, have little artefact evidence associated with them and usually have a commanding position often connected with water, in this case the Devil's Pool/Ditchley Bottom stream (*9*). A number of rectangular square and doubled-ditched enclosures were known to exist within the area as earthworks with low banks, but only one, at the spring near the Lees Rest Farm, had associated artefactual evidence, which was retrieved by metal detecting, indicating a site of ritual significance. Excavations at the site in the 1950s were poorly recorded, though a head of Mercury was retrieved (Linington 1962). However, these square

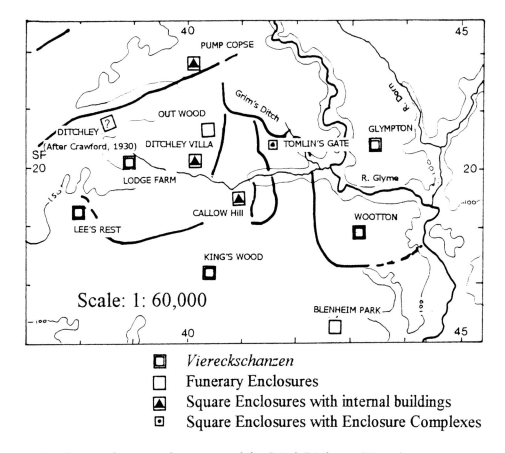

9 Distribution of square enclosures around the Grim's Ditch area (Massey)

features with entrances in just one side can be seen as being places of collective assemblage, and of part-cult and part-political character, expressing the identity of distinctive kinship groups. *Viereckschanzen* also have an affinity with springs and water, especially overlooking rivers, and perhaps the siting of Grim's Ditch between the Glyme and Evenlode are also significant in this aspect.

Massey suggested that the distribution of *Viereckschanzen* appear to be near breaks in the bank and ditch of Phase One of Grim's Ditch and effectively defines the layout of the circuit. What is also significant is that there are two such features on the western bank of the Evenlode opposite ridge, forming the neck of Phase One of Grim's Ditch. When the proposed *Viereckschanzen* at Lee's Rest was excavated it was found that a palisade trench was located in the outer of its two ditches. Such a cross section is very similar to that of the Grim's Ditch Phase One perimeter and may indicate a religious role for the whole enclosure. If this is so then it can be postulated that the earthwork circuit was the socio-religious centre of a much larger area and that its siting is a result of the availability of water, and that trade functions were situated outside the circuit, in this case to the north.

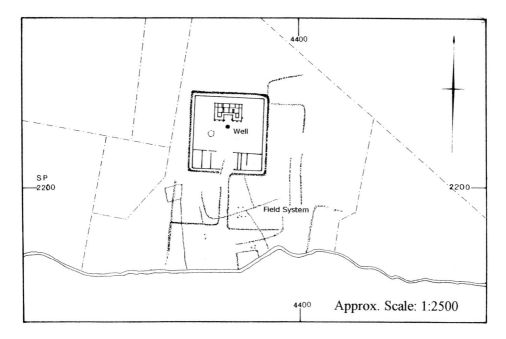

10 Ditchley villa within a *Viereckschanze*-type enclosure (Massey)

Massey also identified smaller, single–ditched enclosures surrounded by large groups of pits as being '*grabgarten*', enclosures for burial, as well as possible 'Gallo–Belgic' type sanctuaries. That there are large numbers of these square enclosures in the area can be detected from the aerial photographs, and are too small to be later villa features.

While some of Massey's interpretation might be seen as ambitious considering the sparse distribution of such a range of enclosures in southern and midland England (though this may be a function of them being unrepresented in the archaeological literature) the conditions for recovery of such features were exceptional and there is no doubt that such a density does exist, and perhaps there may be some of these Continental-type features which survive into Roman-period villas.

Interestingly, the evidence for settlement within the Phase One enclosure is virtually absent except that associated with two later villa sites, those at Ditchley and Callow Hill, both of which have produced large quantities of Gallo-Roman pottery (*10*). It is the site at Ditchley villa above the Devils Pool on the north valley side of the tributary stream of the Glyme, that would appear to be the more important of the two with traces of a banjo enclosure that may be related to a spring that, in times of heavy rain, issues from a point adjacent and immediately east of the site. This later Iron Age site also appears to dominate the springs from which the tributary flows. It has been pointed out by Massey that the shape of a later villa could be interpreted as a stylised banjo enclosure (*11*).

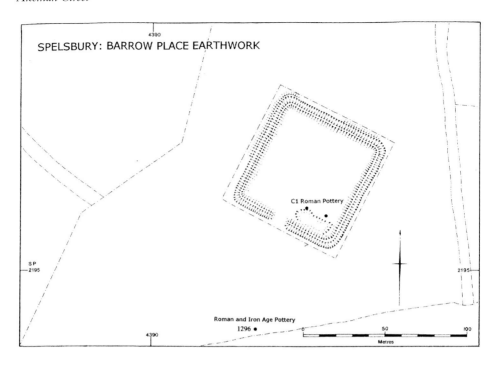

SPELSBURY: BARROW PLACE EARTHWORK

C1 Roman Pottery

S P
—2195

2195—

Roman and Iron Age Pottery
1296 •

0   50   100

Metres

11 Barrow Place earthwork (Massey)

The study of the aerial photographs and fieldwork to identify pottery clusters of the later Iron Age resulted also in the recognition of a dense distribution of settlements to the north of the Grim's Ditch enclosure, between the Glyme and Evenlode, with many of these features producing Gallo-Belgic pottery types and fragments of amphora. To the east of the Dorn and the south of the Grim's Ditch enclosure, traces of settlement proved to be of low density and sporadic.

The labour to construct the perimeter bank and ditch for the 13 sq km of Phase One must have come from a much larger area than that within the complex and this is substantiated by Massey's assessment of the amount of work-time which was needed to construct the complex and will be discussed in the following section. Massey notes that within the territorial block to the north there was evidence of a high degree of clustering of structures which correlated tightly with the location of major settlement enclosures, including large numbers of banjo enclosures which probably ante-dated the Grim's Ditch enclosure, which may provide evidence for the Grim's Ditch being the focus for an elite within a ranked society, and possibly extensive kinship patterns which are reflected in the *Viereckschanzen* in Phase One. Importantly for the Grim's Ditch area the limited evidence from fieldwalking suggests a period of use spanning the first century BC and the early Roman period. Also, there appears to be little mid Iron Age settlement within the Grim's Ditch area and it is likely that the *oppida* was a later Iron Age phenomenon, although probably of short duration, maybe no more time than it took to construct it.

Undoubtedly, the population of these enclosures would have provided the majority of the labour for the construction of the earthwork system and perhaps were represented within the square ditched sites of the Phase One enclosure. The building of the Phase One circuit would have taken decades to complete and is unlikely to have had anything to do with warfare or been built as a direct response to a military threat. That there would have needed to be some sort of social hierarchy that could demand labour tribute in order to be set in motion also has implications for community structures. That both the first and second phases appear to have been built in an *ad hoc* manner might indicate construction over a long period, as tribute to show the power and riches of the elite. Considering the lack of defensive attributes and the period of time necessary to construct the feature, it is likely that the conception of Phase One was halted not because of the presence of the Roman Army, but because the whole concept of tribute needed to be modified in the light of changing socio-economic factors that resulted from the construction of the Roman road of Akeman Street.

To the south of the Phase One earthwork the landscape appears to be empty of crop and soil marks except were there are later villas. These later Iron Age settlements, Fawler, North Leigh and Shakenoak, are all situated in, or directly above, the Evenlode valley on what may be the north-west to south-east trade routes to the Thames valley. That such settlements were to metamorphose into early villas argues for wealth that may well not have only come from the settlement to the north of the first phase of the Grim's Ditch, but also from the Thames valley, and indicates a continuity of identity and power into the Roman period.

The lack of later Iron Age settlement is not only apparent south of Phase One of Grim's Ditch, but also to the west where there are few indications of any occupation until the area of the Bagendon complex, indicating that there was no long-distance route from east to west. The only possibility of settlement for the later Iron Age on the Roman route is at Asthall where a square enclosure was identified from the air close to the road and categorised by Welfare and Swann (1995) as an 'Iron Age type-settlement', but is better seen as a Roman rural site. A banjo enclosure has also been located through aerial photography at North Leach 7km north of the line of the later Akeman Street and its situation is likely to be due to the north-west to south-east valley of the Leach which offers shelter and a trading route (Darvill and Hingley 1982).

THE WELSH WAY

No doubt the inhospitable, windswept high plateau of the Cotswolds discouraged settlement and the first indication of a later Iron Age route is the Welsh Way, or Tame's Way as has since become known, after the Tame family who were rich Cotswold merchants of the seventeenth century. It was the London–Gloucester

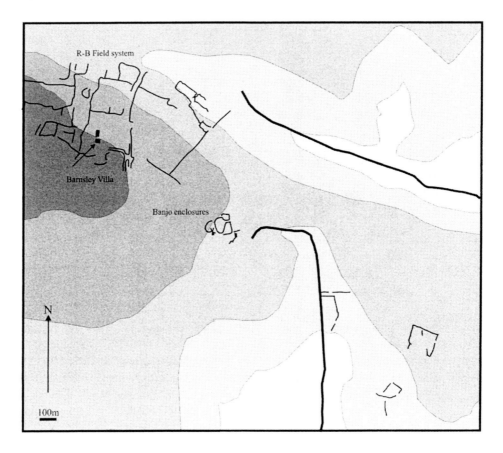

12 Banjo enclosure, Roman villa and field system at Barnsley (Tom Moore)

route during the later Iron Age at least (Witts 1882; Sawyer 1897; Baddeley 1925). The Way can be traced back to the thirteenth century as a drover's route, but the significant factor in its inclusion here is that it connects the route from the River Thames at its highest navigable point at Lechlade with the later Iron Age settlement at Bagendon and then continues on to Gloucester, the lowest crossing point of the River Severn, the Forest of Dean and Welsh Borders beyond. It would appear that the braided nature of the track has led to two recognisable routes, one through Quenington and one through Fairford. Between Barnsley and Bagendon the Welsh Way appears on late seventeenth-century maps as a slightly curved route with straight sections, but since the enclosure of parishes on its route in the mid-eighteenth century there has been some straightening of the track to make it into the present road, though generally the rectangular enclosed fields, road and hedges respect its course, confirming an earlier date.

Barnsley seems to have been an important location on the route, as the accounts of the Rev Charles Coxwell of Barnsley record that on 28 October 1782, he received £1 7s 0d, '... for the use of 3 acres one night for 50 head

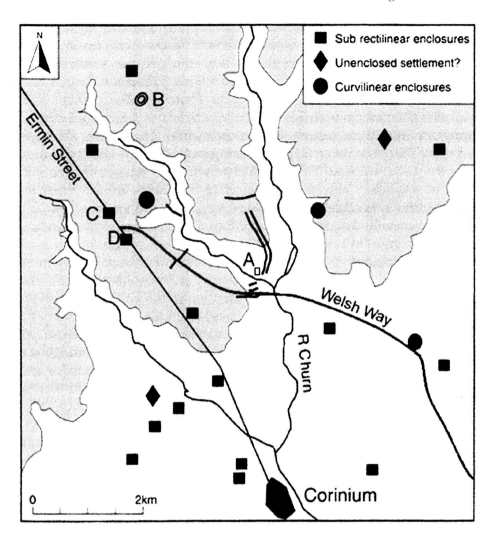

13 The relationship between Corinium, Bagendon, Ditches, the Duntisbournes and the Welsh Way (Cotswold Archaeology)

of Welsh cattle', while on November of the same year he recorded a payment of 12*d*, 'for a small drove of Welsh cattle' (Colyer 1974). Aerial photographic evidence of a banjo enclosure in Barnsley Park suggests that in the later Iron Age the site was significant for the same purposes (*12*). A stone-built set of pre-villa earthworks were located at this point and excavated. This first phase of the Barnsley site had no coins to date it; however, most of the brooches were at the latest from the end of the first century, and others were of types that might well have been earlier. Pottery from the Severn valley might also be earlier than the excavation report suggests. A later Iron Age Western Series silver coin was also found and designated to this phase of the structures. There have been other interpretations of this site which will be discussed in later chapters, but it is possible that this first phase should not be later Iron Age and related in some way to the banjo enclosure.

Coming off the undulating landscape and down into the valley of the Churn, the Welsh Way does a 'dog-leg' to negotiate obliquely the steep slope. At the top of that 'pitch' when at right angles to the River Churn, a view of the Bagendon Brook valley with its later Iron Age earthworks opens out spectacularly. This panorama is clearly designed for maximum effect with the Cultham Lane Dyke, which cannot be seen from the Churn valley bottom, cutting upwards across the contours and the Perrot Brook Dykes demonstrating that the Welsh Way will have to respect the valley bottom by skirting around it (*13*).

THE BAGENDON COMPLEX

The valley of the Bagendon Brook provides the only route through the gently dipping plateau at the southern end of the Cotswolds before the marshy area of the Thames valley is reached near the later site of Cirencester, and it is highly likely that it was in use some time before the later Iron Age occupation. The valley is also fed by springs, which would be essential for cattle in a permeable Oolitic limestone area which was largely lacking in streams. Controlling such a route would be a major political and trading advantage. With the economic importance of the South East and Thames valley, especially in the years before the 'official' conquest in AD 43 when Roman influence was greater than has previously been usually acknowledged, the Welsh Way route was the obvious candidate for trade and control of that economic activity and this may account for the complex of sites in the Bagendon area.

There is a choreographic relationship between the dykes and the valley of the Bagendon Brook (*14*). The nine dykes appear to control movement through and around the valley in a carefully orchestrated manner and this also points to a tight relationship to the sites within the valley. The dykes display little relationship to the contours and do not form an obvious enclosure but effectively delimitate a significant area of 200ha. On the north side of the valley, cutting up through the spur formed by the Churn and its tributary, is a major earthwork, the Culham Lane Dyke, which as it climbs through the contours has two parallel dykes outside it controlling movement into the valley of the brook. On the same side of the valley but sited on the edge of the plateau is the Scrubditch, which although could be interpreted as anomalous because its ditch faces into the valley, may well have been demarcating the northern extent of the designated significant area. The aim of both the Scrubditch and that at Culham Lane may also have had the effect of emphasising the position of an area of very flat contours above the incised valley slope where a possible 'banjo-type' enclosure has been detected from the air (*15*). This could have been clearly seen from the Welsh Way before

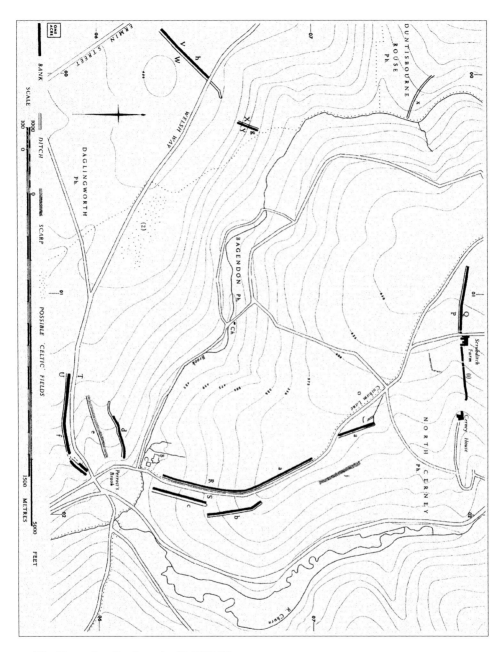

14 The Bagendon Earthworks (RCHME)

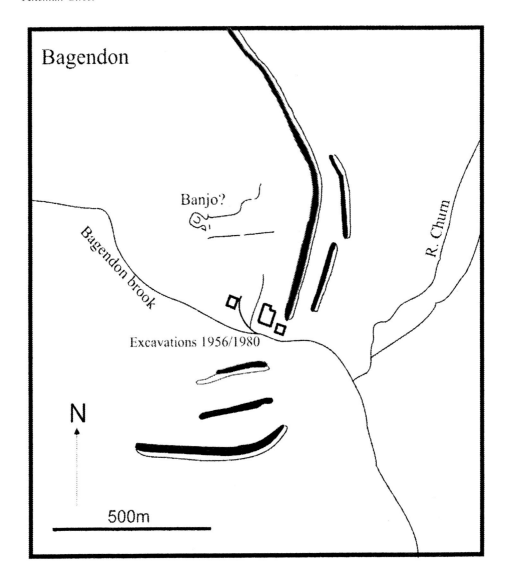

15 Possible banjo enclosure at Bagendon (Tom Moore)

it descended into the valley of the Churn and again as it climbed the hill on the south side of the valley.

Bagendon Brook itself does not have a ditch fronting it, although excavation has detected a road alongside it moving from east to west (Trow 1982). The incised valley has a cross-sectional profile which is steeper on the north side, however, the southern slope offers the possibility of a route climbing diagonally up to the plateau with relative ease on a manageable gradient and this was used by the Welsh Way. On the southern bank are at least two dykes that channel the route obliquely across the contours, which become spaced wider apart with height, until it reaches the plateau and the road in the direction of the River Severn, the Forest of Dean and the South Wales area, broadly following the later Roman road, Ermine Street. Any such route would have brought iron and coal as well as Welsh gold to the South East. It might also be possible that it was the route of May Hill conglomerate rock that was used in the Thames valley as quernstones (Tom Moore 2006a).

The dating of the Bagendon dykes, which define the confluence of the Churn and Bagendon Brook, is uncertain (Courtney and Hall 1984). Only one of them is known to be contemporary with the settlement, but the lack of continuity of the earthworks makes relative dating impossible, although there must be a long interval in between them considering the large amount of labour, and social obligation, needed to build them (Clifford 1961). The settlement behind the dykes may have been short-lived, perhaps 20 years at the most, and is likely to have ceased around AD 60. There may, however, be large areas of inaccessible archaeological deposits below the present Bagendon village and perhaps another high-status structure lies there. Where that labour came from is still uncertain, but does suggest a more extensive settlement complex than can be detected at present. Excavations by Clifford in the 1950s produced evidence of the minting of coins, and possible huts. Mrs Clifford suggested that the site may have been the 'capital' of the Dobunni. Later excavation demonstrated that the site was industrial in nature, and the platform for huts identified earlier was in fact a roadway into the area behind the dykes.

DITCHES

The Ditches site is only 2km from the northernmost dyke and only 3.5km from the occupation site behind the dykes. It appears to have been earlier than the Bagendon Dykes, its construction probably taking place in the first century BC (Trow 1988; Trow S., James, S. and Moore, T. forthcoming). The double-ditched oval enclosure's southern and eastern sides are slightly flattened and a pair of ditches defining a trackway have been detected and led from the entrance at the north-east corner into a dry valley east of the site. To the south-west a curving 'antennae' ditch runs from a second entrance into a second dry valley to the west. Within the enclosure a ditched trackway, abruptly changing direction twice, joins the north-western and south-western entrances. Other features include lengths of ditch and a variety of pit-like features. Its early economy seems to have involved cattle and sheep, and there is also evidence for textile processing. The exact status of the Ditches site in the later Iron Age Bagendon complex is difficult to determine, though the presence of iron currency bars and the possibility of minting gold and silver coins from the production of coin blanks found on the site suggest a high-status occupation.

Ditches' relationship with the Bagendon Dykes has a number of interesting features. They were probably later than the first phase of the Ditches enclosure high above them and the sites are not inter-visible being hidden from each other by a valley spur, a relationship which has echoes of similarity with the lack of visibility between Gorhambury and Prae Wood at Verlamion. If this is the case it can be postulated that the Ditches is earlier, and the Bagendon Dykes may represent a display of power dominating the confluence of the Bagendon Brook with the Churn, as the Ditches site does the upper parts of the valley and the plateau route to the River Severn.

What is important from the point of view of the traveller is that the Ditches site hangs on the edge of the northern valley side above a set of springs and in direct sight of the Welsh Way which climbs obliquely across the southern slope. The Ditches structures could easily be seen as proclaiming where the source of power and wealth lay to the traveller entering or leaving the valley from the north-west. The marshy area at the bottom of the valley must have given Ditches a presence, not only in terms of political dominance, but of potent ritual significance, aspects often being seen as a duality. The relationship with Bagendon itself appears to be that the Ditches was of high-status occupancy and at Bagendon immediately behind the dykes was an area focused on production and, therefore, it is unlikely that there was any competition between the sites. However, the chronological relationship between them is not completely secure.

DUNTISBOURNE GROVE AND MIDDLE DUNTISBOURNE

The Welsh Way meets what was later to become Ermine Street on the col at Dartley Bottom, which represents the last vestiges in the landscape of the Bagendon Brook. On either side of the 'saddle' are the sites of Duntisbourne Grove and Middle Duntisbourne, facing one another. At Middle Duntisbourne the area enclosed may have been about 0.6ha though no features were found within that area. The occupation seemed to have comprised of two phases; there is little dating evidence for the first phase, though the second phase could be dated to the end of the Iron Age or very early Roman period (Mudd *et al.* 1999). The Duntisbourne Grove site produced a sub-rectangular enclosure at least 180m (north–south) by at least 110m (east–west), and a little over 2ha in area. Again there was no surviving evidence of structures or occupation within the enclosure, though only approximately ten per cent was excavated. It was suggested that there were two phases of occupation, followed by abandonment, and the sequence of events occupied a relatively brief period within the first century AD. The size of the ditches varied, being only 1.4m deep on the downhill side but up to 2.6m deep on the eastern side. Since the enclosure occupied an elevated but not easily defended position, because of higher ground to the south and south-east, it was unlikely to be primarily for defence, if at all. Since the deepest ditch and presumably a higher bank were on the eastern side, very close to the route of the Welsh Way as it crests the ridge, perhaps these features were designed to impress and demonstrate surveillance or synonymously announce high status to the traveller moving out of the Bagendon Brook valley. Although throughout this 'journey' through the Bagendon complex it has appeared that the iconography was designed to impress/control the traveller coming from east to west, the structures at Duntisbourne Grove may have had the same function as that at Gorhambury, with ditches and banks lower on the plateau side so that the structures inside the enclosure might be seen from a distance and so signal power through height to those coming up the hill.

The excavators considered the two structures, both producing high-status imports and amphora, to be part of the same settlement. With both Bagendon and the Ditches being only 2.5km to the south-east and north-east respectively, the extended site may be part of the 'complex'. Unlike Bagendon and Ditches, this site has produced a high quantity of pork bones which may be indicative of a woodland, or edge of woodland, environment. The excavation report hinted at the connection between high-status sites and woodland, which suggests a shrine or religious role in which case an important part of a poly-focal settlement might have been located at the point where the Welsh Way leaves the valley and continues north-west.

The link between all these sites is the importation of high-status Continental pottery, but since both Ditches and Bagendon have seen much more excavation it is possible to see parallels between them. The artefactual evidence demonstrates close relationships between the two sites, especially the first-century coarse pottery with many forms and fabrics being common, and also objects associated with textile processing as well as bone tools and iron objects. There are also connections between the Duntisbourne sites and both Ditches and Bagendon in terms of fine Gaulish and other tablewares.

Pottery assemblages included Arretine and South Gaulish Samian forms, Terra-Rubbra and Terra-Nigra as well as amphora fragments possibly of Spanish origin, indicating long-term elite trade. Both Ditches and Bagendon used fine glassware, large quantities of British coins and a wide range of brooches. As a result of fieldwalking around the Ditches site a probable later Iron Age conquest Augustan intaglio has been found, demonstrating that the site had a well-developed network of trade connections. What Bagendon and Ditches share, though so far there has been no evidence from the Duntisbournes, is evidence for the minting of coins, though as yet the date and dedicatee(s) are not known. What also seems to be shared between the sites is a short yet intense period of activity, reflected in the Bagendon Dykes and the Duntisbourne sites from their origin to abandonment. Ditches also shares in this activity, even though the features associated with it have been truncated by further development or ploughing, or have not yet been excavated.

CIRENCESTER

Later Iron Age occupation at Cirencester is apparent in a series of farms overlooking the later town site, and preceding the Roman fort period a circle of stake holes and possibly a stake palisade found adjacent to the Verulamium Gate. Cirencester demonstrates similar features to Verlamion – the marshy nature of the River Churn and the need to canalise it in the Roman period might indicate that this is another part of the 'Bagendon' landscape as a shrine of some sort.

The idea of a 'proto' Roman Akeman Street has not proved to be as straightforward as has been thought – the later Iron Age route does not appear to have been just 'given the full treatment' and this opens up further dilemmas: the function(s) of the route of the later Iron Age routeways, the nature of the *oppida* the road supposedly joined, and whether there were any consolidated tribal blocks with well-defined boundaries between them – all of these issues being central to our understanding of the role of Roman Akeman Street in the landscape, and of the landscape in relation to the importance of the road. It is the location, history and function of the *oppida* that appear to be the crucial factors in the landscape, and their related issues of tribes, tribal territories, coinage and eventually continuities of the development and function of the Roman *civitates* and their capitals.

4

PRE-ROMAN AKEMAN STREET: *OPPIDA,* TRIBES AND IDENTITIES

Was there a pre-Roman Akeman Street? The way that individuals and communities positioned themselves close to, and were positioned by, movements of a wide range of products such as precious metals, cattle, slaves, and reciprocally new forms of high-status pottery and wine, is the important factor in considering why it is unlikely that there was a pre-Roman Akeman Street. Not only were links in terms of trade and goods originating on the Continent important, but also the range of ideas carried by traders or perhaps brought back to the British mainland by mercenaries and the sons of prominent individuals who had social and political connections with Rome (Creighton 2006). These interactions, experiences and possibilities that began to change the identities of the elites in the later Iron Age along the subsequent course of Akeman Street. Unfortunately, many of the factors that might explain further what was happening along the river valleys are highly contentious, but cannot be understood without a perspective based on movement, mobility and the creation of individual and group identities.

THE THREE '*OPPIDA*'

Early Roman Akeman Street is intimately connected with Verlamion, the North Oxfordshire Grim's Ditch and Bagendon, and it is not possible to understand later developments throughout the Roman period unless the individual characteristics and trajectories of development of the three entities and their wider relationships are examined in some detail. There has been an ongoing debate about this type of site's role in the landscape, its relationship to consolidated tribes with distinct territories, the definition of borders around it, and the distribution of tribal coinages in relation to all three issues (Moore, T. and Reece, R. 2001).

The term '*oppida*' is a highly fraught one, and it is not at all helpful to compare these settlements with those on the Continent from where the term has been transposed onto the large British earthwork-delineated settlement sites (Woolf 1993). Certainly, some of the features of these mainland European settlements are identifiable in British examples, for example in evidence for poly-focal functions such as religious, industrial and domestic areas, but in Britain these can be spread over a very wide area, and are usually outside the main enclosure. So, although the term will be used here because it is a familiar one, it has to be expected that like 'henges' or 'hillforts' there will be differences in appearance, if not function, and that our understanding of this class of features as well its individual examples is still developing.

Unfortunately, all of the sites suffer from lack of recent excavation with nearly everything known about the details of these individual entities having come from archaeological interventions before the 1960s and in some cases the 1930s. In such large present-day agricultural areas plough damage has been responsible for the destruction of earthworks and sites, which has caused problems with both determining aspects of their function and their dating, so there is a significant challenge in comparing like with like. In understanding such large complexes much depends on fieldwork rather than excavation to elucidate the size of the area and the varying functions of blocks of settlement and this has been undertaken by Hunn (1992) at Verlamion and Copeland (1998) and Massey (1999) on the Grim's Ditch. Because the Bagendon complex is much dispersed, or of a completely different nature, large-scale work across the landscape has not been possible. The Grim's Ditch area has been more fruitful in providing evidence of the settlement surrounding the main *oppida* enclosure because of the soil characteristics which produce clear cropmarks in the right conditions, whereas the sites of the other two monuments do not have this advantage; but the lack of identified sites does not mean that they are not present in the landscape awaiting discovery.

MOVEMENT AND THE POSITION OF *OPPIDA*

Verlamion, the Grim's Ditch and Bagendon all appear to have been founded in areas where there was no, or little, previous mid or late Iron Age settlement activity. These types of sites have been described as 'liminal', on the edge of, or between other groups of longer-established communities which have mid or late Iron Age characteristics (Moore 2006). This 'liminality' might be the result of new systems of exchange being set up that did not fit into the settlement patterns of traditional 'down the line' trade, possibly because of the growing volume of commerce with the Continent in the period of *c*.AD 10-40 and this may

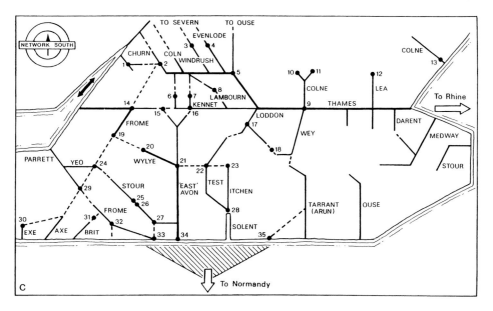

16 Trade networks in the later Iron Age (after Sherratt). 2 indicates the site of Bagendon, 4 the North Oxfordshire Grim's Ditch and 11 Verlamion.

have initiated a different direction and function of movement in the landscape. Incomers, with a much more developed understanding of the geography of the longer routes and how they could be used for trading, may well have followed these combined short-distance routes back to their eventual destinations, finding suitable sites for their own exchange activities where they might act as 'brokers' between trade routes and commodities. As such these sites are situated near the confluences of rivers. There does not appear to be any evidence for coercion in the design of the resulting *oppida* and this is probably because no one was displaced by the new arrangements. Indeed there might have been an attraction for the peoples of the wider region because of the opportunity of increased trade possibilities with local produce being moved alongside more precious commodities. In this way the settlements and the social obligations grew in size and location.

The location of each *oppida* is associated with clearly delineated north–west/south–east routes following river valleys across the landscape (Sherratt 1996) (*16*). It is clearly apparent that a major South Wales/Forest of Dean/River Severn route determined the site of Bagendon, and the site of North Oxfordshire Grim's Ditch by the Cherwell north–south route as well as routes coming from the West Midlands. The discreteness of these routes has been argued because of the absence of later Iron Age settlement between the North Oxfordshire Grim's Ditch and Bagendon which may be a result of lack of fieldwork and difficulties with aerial photography; however, there is an equal lack of Roman settlement except that related to the road or very near it. This is not to say that there were not minor routes between them, but a major route does go across the grain of the landscape. Again there is a lack of contemporary settlement between the Grim's Ditch and Bierton/Aylesbury as the Vale of Aylesbury has produced very few artefacts or sites. The proposed Bierton/Aylesbury later Iron Age complex is as much aligned with trade from the Northamptonshire area into the Chiltern Gap at Tring and then to Verlamion or south to Maidenhead as it is to the west along Akeman Street.

One thing that is likely to be highly significant is that each of these large earthwork complexes was on a tributary of the River Thames and was connected eventually with the South East, Gaul and the Iberian peninsular and this could have been an important factor in the choice of site. However, in the case of Bagendon there may also have been a trade connection with the River Severn and Bristol Channel, and Gloucester at the lowest crossing point would have been a very valuable location for a later Iron Age settlement. Indeed, if this was the case then it might explain the lack of development of the Bagendon area and the position of the early Roman Kingsholm fortress.

It is difficult to say what function river transport had in the regions. Each of the major rivers, Evenlode, Cherwell and Ver, were probably navigable by flat-bottomed craft, at least seasonally, and this might have aided trade into the Thames valley and its eventual links with the sea. Bagendon was some way from the Thames and the Churn was not navigable even with the highest water levels in winter. There is no reason why water transport might also be possible, in that some suitable cargoes were transferred from land to streams, again with seasonal factors being important. The presence at Bagendon of Continental imports of pottery could as easily be an artefact of trade along the Thames, communications with the River Severn, or as likely, the movement of goods from the south coast. Similarly, objects which appear to originate in the Camulodunum or the Verlamion area could have been brought by water transport or have been traded in other ways rather than directly through a link from the North Oxfordshire Grim's Ditch westwards. Just as there is a close correlation between pottery manufacturing and rivers in the Roman period because of the bulky nature of the cargo, this may well have been the same with pottery from eastern England or further afield.

OPPIDA MOVEMENT AND DESIGN

Each of these three large ditched and expansive settlements, although they are all likely to be early to mid first century AD, were dynamic, having different roles at different dates. However, they did not have parallel temporalities, and certainly have different trajectories of development. It is known that each of the sites were eventually influenced by Roman power, but again it is hard to say whether they were contemporaneous with each other or not, and certainly the outcomes of this relationship were very different. These different roles are perhaps reflected in their sizes: Verlamion 600 sq m, the North Oxfordshire Grim's Ditch Phase I 13 sq km, Bagendon 600 sq m. Although Verlamion appears to be the same size as Bagendon, the physical situation and type of structures related to it are very different, the former being also archaeologically better known. However, there do seem to be common factors between each of the three sites, though this may not represent a common origin of the builders but the result of wider influences. This is certainly the case with the three examples along 'pre-Roman' Akeman Street where there are very few structures actually inside the banks and ditches bounding the enclosure, where an enclosure can be identified. This may indicate also that the linear dyke systems were not for defence as there could not be a rapid response to conflict, with their construction taking many years, if not decades, and they were probably part of a social ritual. It would appear therefore that the land inside the dyke systems had other specific functions which seem connected with an elite, while also having a communal aspect – they represent a hierarchical society. However, the elite status that is usually connected with these large monuments can also be seen at smaller sites. If the importation of Gallo-Belgic pottery is taken as an indicator of elite status, then it may be that smaller ditched sites such as Aylesbury/Bierton, which are of the same broad date as the major *oppida*, share some of the same functions.

In the wider landscape *oppida* were situated between blocks of mid to late Iron Age settlement in the early to mid first century AD. It appears that factors such as the presence of water or marshy ground for social and ritual purposes determined the specific localities in valleys which satisfied these needs. While the resulting earthworks were not defensive, they appear to have had a demarcating function, possibly separating sacred from domestic activity, defining status, and in both cases restricting vision into an area. The use of the earthwork profile of bank and ditch (and palisade in the case of the Grim's Ditch) is a development of other forms of demarcation such as of hillforts which also may share some of the *oppida* functions. At Bagendon, with its steeply incised valley, the use of earthworks in this manner may not have been necessary. Using banks and ditches to restrict access visually appears to be not only from the outside but reciprocally from the inside as well. In the case of Verlamion it is quite clear that the position of the banks in front of the Prae Wood settlement made it invisible from the valley, the earthworks appearing to be a extension of the hillside slope, which in turn necessitated the ditches behind the banks being kept clean so that spoil eroded from the bank could be replaced. Ensuring that the height of the bank remained constant may well have given continuity to the social obligation of the inhabitants of the Prae Wood enclosure. Similarly perhaps, the North Oxfordshire Grim's Ditch sequence of bank, ditch and outer palisade may have had a similar function, acting as a screen to activities inside. In both cases the linearity of the ditched systems are well adapted to the landscape, following contours around the valley, except for the stretches that close up the valley at one end and the earthworks cut across the contours. Again, at Bagendon this may not have been necessary due to the steepness of the valley. At the Grim's Ditch however, the ditch appears to have been filled in shortly after construction, possibly because of a change in function of the area and this is also the case with the Bagendon dykes.

There is little evidence for settlement within the enclosures at any of the sites, except for the central enclosure at Verlamion and some banjo enclosures within the Grim's Ditch, although the site of Ditchley villa may have been important as is discussed below. As yet there is no evidence for a ritual core at Bagendon. Each of the sites seem to have a high-status structure dominating it – Gorhambury, Callow Hill and Ditches for Verlamion, the Grim's Ditch and Bagendon respectively with the first two being associated with breaks in the earthworks enclosing the space. Each *oppida* has produced Gallo-Roman pottery which has been found by both fieldwalking and excavation. Bagendon, Ditches and Verlamion have both produced clay slab moulds which are usually associated with coin manufacture, though there is no evidence of the authority striking them.

Outside the ditched and banked core of Verlamion at Prae Wood, and north of the Grim's Ditch, were what would appear to be settlement in hierarchical distributions. The burials at King Harry Lane and the *Viereckschanzen* and *grabgarten* at the Grim's Ditch, both inside the earthwork enclosure, emphasise this relationship and this will be discussed in more detail below. The Duntisbourne sites at the head of the Bagendon valley may have had the same hierarchical layering but evidence for ritual sites associated with it is lacking at present.

MOVEMENT AND MOBILITY INSIDE THE *OPPIDA*

Each of these *oppida* appear to have controlled routes for movement within their enclosed areas. At the beginning of this chapter a route through Verlamion and its implications for travellers and settlers were choreographed and it would seem that banks and ditches were responsible for imposing specific lines of movement through a central area. Whether these routes were for outsiders or communal mobility is not known. It may well be that traders were diverted elsewhere outside the enclosures, but this then divorces the economic aspects from the *oppida*. The route into the valley of the Ver was planned to ensure that the Gorhambury structures, a possible square six-post structure which was replaced by a circular hut, were seen as overlooking the valley and its routes, and also that the central enclosure could be seen but not entered. Perhaps the Fosse had a palisade, or was high enough to completely block the view inside. The presence of the Fosse and White Dykes moved the eyes from Gorhambury to the central enclosure in an almost processional manner. The central enclosure would have been recognised immediately as a centre of ritual power because of its relationship with the river and the marsh. It would be expected that selected dead of the community would have been buried within the sacred/community area of the *oppida*. It is very likely that the most economically important route was from the Cow Roast direction, bringing goods that were transported on to Camulodunum and therefore prestigious and wealth-giving to the elites of the Verlamion *oppida* reinforcing their privileged position. A view down into the valley with its visually powerful structures would have emphasised this.

A similar arrangement can be seen at the North Oxfordshire Grim's Ditch. The main settlement blocks are outside the banks and ditch, with possibly a palisade to hinder the view from inside out. If Ditchley was the main focus of the *oppida*, then Callow Hill may have been the 'gate-keeper', the 'Gorhambury-type' site. From the Callow Hill entrance, which can be seen from the Ditchley site, a ditch and bank funnels movement through the Phase One area. The pre-Ditchley villa site can also be seen from this route which would then appear to move to the north-west past the Lees Rest site. Again, the ritual aspect in the guise of the *Viereckschanzen* is encompassed with the earthwork circuit, and these structures have connections with Gallo-Roman practices, which may have some connection with the design of the later Ditchley villa. Phase One of the North Oxfordshire Grim's Ditch is much bigger than the area of Verulamium and there may be more features to be found. The Prae Wood equivalent settlement is found to the north of the enclosed area, invisible from the valley in which Ditchley lies.

Bagendon is in a completely contrasting locality. A 'gatekeeper' site demonstrating power and prestige appears to be at Ditches site high above the Bagendon Brook. Although both Gorhambury and Callow Hill are located to be easily visible, the profile of the Bagendon valley determined the windswept position of Ditches. The central core of the Bagendon complex has not been recognised but may lie under the present village or be associated with the springs below the Ditches site. Considering the presence of pig bones at the Duntisbournes it is possible that the ritual site was there. The Welsh Way as the major route through the complex is connected to each of these sites visually. However, there is no need for the Bagendon complex to have had the same configuration as the other two *oppida* as it was in a totally different physical environment and may well have been founded by a group with a completely different social system. Each of the gatekeeper sites seems to have been abandoned in the late third century, and this may well reflect the transfer of sites of memory and power to other features.

Bagendon has been described as the private park of an elite based at Ditches with a later settlement behind the dykes and because of the different configuration from other examples of *oppida* (Reece 1990). It would appear that there are some similarities of design between each of the sites discussed, but there are significant differences also. All three could be described as 'private estates' of elites and just as medieval villages were often associated with, but out of sight of, the sites of power in the manor house, the church was also near the latter because of the connection between the political and sacred, and often hunting estates were enclosed within park pales of banks with ditches on the inside.

OPPIDA **AND PEOPLE**

In the later Iron Age individuals and communities are archaeologically invisible along what was to become Roman Akeman Street, except within the wider *oppida* surroundings as well as in some of the banjo-type enclosures around Alchester and at iron-working sites in the Bulbourne valley, both of which it could be argued were related to the *oppida*. However, possibly because of this clustering around the large banked and ditched demarcated sites, the sense of commitment and social obligation of such groups can be seen well in the construction of both phases of the earthworks of the large, ditched enclosure of the North Oxfordshire Grim's Ditch, and presumably this was continued unchanged as their descendants became the first- and second-century rural populations along the Roman road and were responsible for the non-*oppida* Phase Two circuit.

Massey (1999) undertook an exercise in assessing how much settler-power the North Oxfordshire Grim's Ditch system would have taken to build, and although such attempts are fraught with difficulties, his results do give an insight into how extensive the system was and how it related to social relationships with the area around it in terms of the available labour required for its construction. To build the entire perimeter, bank and ditch of both phases, he considers would have involved a total labour input of 5,328,000 person hours. Considering the variable morphology of the circuit, some elements using remodelled natural features, and gaps in the earthworks, Massey has calculated that this might reasonably be reduced to 3,500,000 person hours, but this excludes the construction of a continuous timber palisade and the activities of felling and transporting the timber, or the digging of turf to rivet the rampart as was suggested above. Massey suggests that the available dating evidence from pottery (which is a very small and often indeterminate sample) indicates that the construction of the entire complex must have taken place over much more than two decades and quite possibly less. For this activity, Massey assumes a construction sequence extending over 20 years and calculates that if a 10 hour day during the summer months is a reasonable proposition, the annual labour requirement of 175,000 person hours would be required. Where is this labour coming from, and what are the social obligations that are being satisfied by this construction? There is certainly plentiful settlement immediately to the north of Phase One of Grim's Ditch, but it is unlikely that this would have been enough. This presents a pattern of packed centres of relatively even distribution of between 3 and 4km intervals and reveals a series of conjectural territorial divisions of approximately 15-20 sq km. This clustering also appears to correlate with the location of major settlement enclosures which may be identified as centres of high settlement density, so that a series of ranked concentrations of between two and ten settlements per square kilometre could be identified and was no doubt part of the source of the labour needed to construct both phases of the North Oxfordshire Grim's Ditch. The discovery at some of these sites of amphora as well as wheel-made 'Aylesford' types of pottery and Gallo-Belgic wares indicates that elite groups also lived in this northern area. It is also worth considering that the two phases had different social and economic mechanisms for providing labour, and that the settlements of the Thames valley, which were possibly part of the wider Grim's Ditch territory, might have provided a considerable workforce from some of it slaves.

Massey identified a large number of sites of ritual significance, *Viereckschanzen*, within Phase One of North Oxfordshire's Grim's Ditch (here being seen as contemporary with Verlamion) several of which still have traces above ground, being protected either by woodland or parkland. They also have an affinity with springs and water, particularly rivers and perhaps the siting of the Grim's Ditch between the Glyme and Evenlode is also significant in this aspect. If this is so then it can be postulated that the earthwork circuit was the socio-religious centre of a much larger area and that the construction of the ditches was also an act of ritual, connected to the demarcation of the area in which the shrines were situated.

This has many echoes of the layout at Verlamion with the cemeteries being separated from the populations who built them by dykes, and being in an area considered to be socio-religious. However, the small area enclosed by dykes and the length of those earthworks at Verlamion, indicate a smaller population and an area of less power.

At Verlamion, the King Harry cemetery, dated *c*.AD 10-40/50, may also reflect the organisation of society (*17*). Two factors are indicative of this: graves at the centre of the cemetery form a cluster of burials and contained abnormally large numbers of grave goods, so perhaps the number of goods deposited was proportional to the number attending the funeral and may be related to the size of the social network in which the deceased lived. Imported goods might reflect long-distance alliances or have enabled mourners to decide on inheritance of power. Secondly, those buried in clusters which were enclosed differed from those buried on the perimeter of the cemetery area. The enclosed clusters generally encircled a large primary grave seen as the founder of the group. Each such group arguably represents a separately defined social unit – those buried outside the enclosure clusters were outsiders not linked to any of the separate groups (Stead and Rigby 1989).

Growth of the cemetery with the addition of new enclosures during the first 50 years of the first century AD symbolises the nucleation of the *oppidum* with each burial enclosure related to a single social group which in life occupied its own residential enclosure. Throughout time the proportion of individual burials outside the enclosed clusters grew suggesting that there was an increasing socially embedded element to the population that had migrated from elsewhere as individuals rather than social groups, who had taken advantage of greater social mobility in early years of the conquest. So, overall decline in grave assembly size can be seen to reflect a decreasing social network as the *oppidum* developed and the place of extended kinship was replaced by the day-to-day contact that is vital for interaction in a decentralised society.

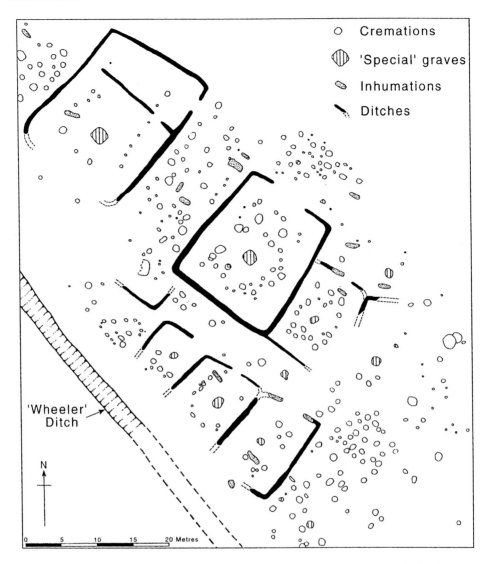

17 Plan of the late Iron Age cemetery at King Harry Lane. *Courtesy of Rosalind Niblett, drawing by David Williams*

MOVEMENT THROUGH TRIBAL TERRITORIES

Because *oppida* look so self-contained behind their banks it is easy to overlook that they were in fact the nexus of economic, social and political perspectives, each of which imply mobility of people and ideas, and that it is through the meeting of these perspectives that *oppida* obtained their meaning. *Oppida* were the centres of trade, they had an elite, there was an important ritual element in what they represented, yet they have been described as being 'no man's land', 'entrepots of trade' and 'gateway communities', all of which underplay their importance in roles other than trade. Another more expansive way of looking at the role of *oppida* in the wider social landscape is that the significant individuals in the *oppida* were members of many communities, possessing multi-memberships, and they needed to build trust with these communities in the immediate area, and at a distance, for trading purposes (Wenger 1998). This is a very different conception from that looking back in time from the Roman *civitas* capitals of Verulamium and Corinium, which were both on the route of Akeman Street, and presuming that these *oppida* were tribal capitals.

Until recently tribal territories have often been thought of as consolidated and cohesive blocks of related peoples with sophisticated hierarchical structures. Roman Akeman Street moved through the Roman *civitates* of the Catuvellauni and the Dobunni, but did it have an influence before *c.*AD 100 when these Roman *civitates* seem to have been formed? We have seen how difficult it is to talk about a later Iron Age Akeman Street, but is there evidence for at least the section from Verlamion to the North Oxfordshire Grim's Ditch crossing tribal boundaries, and if so what implications would this have? Another of the problems of looking at *oppida* as tribal capitals is that they lack the temporal dimension which is crucial in defining identities. Perhaps rather than thinking about *where* the Dobunni and the Catuvellauni were we should be thinking of not just one entity but several, and ask about *when* they were. It might be that the *when* is as important as the *where*, as the composition of social and political groups could have varied through time by amalgamations through marriage and other social forces.

The Catuvellauni have been seen as emerging from a number of small tribes in South Buckinghamshire and South Hertfordshire at about the time of Caesar and having a premier chief, or overall 'king', with the political and economic administration focused very heavily on the tribe's south-eastern quarter in the territory between Camulodunum and Verlamion (Branigan 1985). It was the south-east of the 'kingdom' which was a magnet for agricultural and other wealth in tribute and trade with tribal mobility and petty chiefs living in either nucleated settlements or on large estates. The *oppida* of Verlamion and Camulodunum, in this view, can easily be identified as south-eastern large centres, but where are the settlements of the petty chiefs with their estates? Clearly a pre-Akeman Street routeway would also have been important in the communications between some of these smaller entities but only one possible centre, Bierton in the Vale of Aylesbury has been identified as such.

The identification of the Dobunni makes similar assumptions. It has been stated that it can safely be presumed that there was a *broad* political entity calling itself by that name at the time of the Roman Invasion of AD 43 and that this entity was adopted as a unit of territory by Roman legal administrators (Cunliffe 2003). The adjective 'broad' implies a confederation which would have been composed of a number of different polities and again, the problem is in identifying the settlements that formed this conglomeration of peoples in order to make a political whole with common cultural identities demonstrated in some way, perhaps through artefacts, that could identify the limits of such territories.

Darvill (2003) has proposed that since both the Roman tribal 'cantons' have many river valleys based on the tributaries of major rivers such as the Thames and Severn, we may wish to consider the possibilities of ancestral lands being based on the catchments of these valleys, with the configuration of these territories changing over time. Each of these groups could have been self-contained with plentiful resources in each tributary basin area, and this would not have necessitated inter-area communication and therefore, in such circumstances, it would have been unlikely that fixed inter-tribal hierarchies could develop. However, there could have been some sorts of shared experience. With the ancestral development of different communities there still would have been shared histories and shared artefacts from traders. The final political entity in some of the territories might have been seen as the 'outsiders' who forged the long-distance trade routes and were responsible for the *oppida*-type settlements, and as a multi-member of many of these individual communities, have given more economic coherence to the area. The individual *oppida* may have been the last of the pre-Roman configurations of local or regional settlement and responsible for the latest patterns of movement in a region. However, it would still be possible that some of the populations within an area may well have kept to a mid Iron Age cultural 'package' rather than adopting to that being brought in from outside the area.

Not only do we have to examine the temporality of the separate communities within a region, but also the ways in which they might have related to each other as, for example, 'Dobunni' or 'Catuvellauni', labels which may be the result of Roman administrative policy only. Creating a monolithic tribal area, such as the Romans did, and we continue to do, misses the interaction of individual localities through opportunity for, and the experience of, movement and mobility.

Even if a 'tribe' such as the Dobunni existed it would not be necessary that:

i) all constituencies knew each other well – the more isolated or distant they were the more they would appear to be a *personal* network or one with very limited movements and a set of inter-related practices
ii) everything local communities did was accountable to an overarching elite
iii) everything that each of the local communities used needed to be produced within a particular area of movement reflecting the identity of the wider group.

Unfortunately, the indicators of these local or regional identities, such as having family members in common, is lacking because they are of a social nature and not often reflected in the archaeological record as material objects or sites. Using pottery types has been seen as an indicator of tribal identity, but this is just as likely to have been the influence of marketing areas. It may be that we can approach the problem from a different angle not by looking for similarities but by looking for differences, trying to locate edges of territories marked by borders.

TRIBAL BORDERS

Clearly related to the concept of the tribe, and later the *civitas* capitals joined by Akeman Street, is the existence of tribal borders. Akeman Street has been credited with crossing the margins of the Dobunni and Catuvellauni at Tackley on the River Cherwell, the river being seen as halfway between Bagendon and Verlamion, and the division also based on coin distributions. However, more recently the presence of earthworks, particularly Aves Ditch, being used to define boundaries has also been explored. Before either of these options are considered it is useful to examine the concept of borders in a social context, as this will be related to both the organisation of tribes and the siting of *oppida*. It is important to state at the outset that this discussion can only relate to a possible tribal boundary in a specific place, in this case the Cherwell valley, as patterns elsewhere will have been influenced by totally different circumstances in totally different environments.

There are two types of 'edge' – boundaries and peripheries – which form points of contact with other communities (Wenger 1998). Each emphasises different aspects of movement and identity. Boundaries seem to emphasise discontinuities, lines separating inside from outside, inclusion and exclusion, comfort and vulnerability, the routes moving through them monitored and most of all related to strong central blocks of political units. Most activity along boundaries will be about sustaining them, through addressing conflicts for example. Peripheries emphasise overlap and connections and thus continuities and there is no need for a specific boundary enterprise to sustain them. Being on a periphery means being neither fully inside nor fully outside and indicates a degree of permeability, with a gradient from the core of a community to the extreme periphery and associative in nature rather than controlled. Such points of contact favour meeting places as an opportunity for participation, in the case of *oppida*, between established populations and incomers, from the 'community centre' to the outlying constellations of settlements. The problem is finding evidence for these types of borders in areas where the archaeological evidence is thin, especially as any 'edges' might be a mix of both boundaries and peripheries along a single line.

The Cherwell tribal border proposal is largely numismatic: the distribution of coinage indicates a firm line with little overlap between the coins of the Catuvellauni and the Dobunni (Allen 1944, 1961). From this point everything else follows: the tribal territories, the Aves Ditch earthwork as a boundary, and the boundaries of the Roman *civitates* of the Dobunni and Catuvellauni. Underlying the coinage argument is the fact that the Western Series of coins correspond to the tribal area of the Dobunni and were struck by rulers. Finds of the Western Series of coins appeared to thin out at the Cherwell boundary, therefore, logically, the territory of the Dobunni ends there also. However in the 1990s and before, the incidence of discovered coins might have indicated that the distributions roughly demonstrated a possible relationship between tribal entities and the

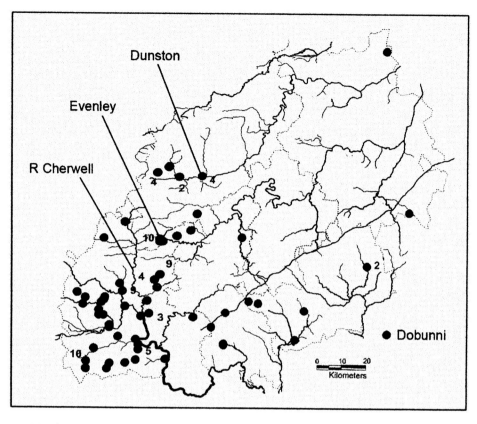

18 Distribution of Dobunnic coins in the area of the Cherwell valley *(after Curteis)*

Cherwell, though many of the finds had been mainly accidental or from sporadic excavations on known sites.

Since that period metal detectorists have been examining the areas around the Cherwell with some energy, often spurred on by publication of reports of archaeological fieldwork. In case studies of three of the four counties through which Akeman Street travelled it has been shown that any border between the two postulated entities of the Dobunni and Catuvellauni was much more blurred than had been previously suggested, a periphery rather than a boundary with Western Serics coins having been found in some abundance at Evenley and Duston, the former being some 9km west of the Cherwell and the latter 30km west of the river (Curteis 2006). What is also interesting is that these coins are found at temple sites and markets, which may indicate peripheries in socially marginalised areas. Although metal detectorists have also been active on the west side of the Cherwell there has been no increase in the number of Catuvellaunian coins (*18*).

Clearly, there must be caveats to these results. Many areas are inaccessible for research because of woodland and permanent pasture. There is also a 'word of mouth factor' in that metal detectorists can find 'honey-pot' sites and search them rigorously while other less promising sites are left unexplored. Much also depends on whether finds are being reported, as if they aren't then not only does the wider distribution pattern become less representative, but the density of finds at sites such as Evenely are under-represented. Of course, areas may be 'blank' because of the lack of later Iron Age settlement. A further consideration, but one that has been overstressed, is the subsequent curation of coins as curiosities by members of the Roman Army, or the coins' use as currency because of their equivalent size to scarce Roman values. So when 13 Western Series coins have been found in the Alchester area it might be argued that this large number was due to the presence of the early Roman military establishment rather than the collection indicating a locality of some later Iron Age importance.

In spite of these possible limitations what is significant about the finds distribution is that these Western Series issues are all late ones (VA 1042-1, 1074-1, 1135-1, 1137-1) and their main distribution is in West Oxfordshire with 20 being found in the North Oxfordshire Grim's Ditch area, another 10 at Evenley and 11 at the headwaters of the Ouse valley around Duston. A coin trail of similarly later issues, from Hereford and Worcester down the Cherwell and into the North Oxfordshire Grim's Ditch, might reflect routes of either political or economic importance. With a little audacity, a trail might even be postulated along pre-Roman Akeman Street as there are incidences of later Dobunnic coins in the Aylesbury/Beirton areas and also at St Albans.

The role of coinage is hotly debated, but here it is taken as a way of encouraging social obligation, a return for certain items or services and not as a medium of exchange. So, find spots are important, but more powerful if their movements to those places can be explained along with the implications of this for cultural identity. Coinage in these terms is about circulation of power and its relationships and developing relationships. Coinage is indicative of the complexity of political relationships and long-distance trade flows, and although find spots are important, it is the movement to those points and the reasons for this mobility that are equally as crucial. Within such a series of cultural practices there are a number of ways in which coinage can be defined, depending on the social context in which it is used. Coinage in the form of high-value coins has malleability, a capacity to take on different forms and modes of exchange depending on its use. It has different systems of symbolic meaning in relation to movement and mobility, so that the function of coinage is transformed from one social situation to the next. Specifically if *oppida* were locations for brokering goods and ideas, then the elite would need legitimacy in order to be a multi-member of several social groups. Coinage especially might provide this legitimacy and the coinage would be possibly backed by ritual which makes it an even more potent system.

Translating between the different facets of movement activities requires codes and conventions, and within the territorialisation of everyday life, this depends on whether some sort of stable set of social identities needs to be established or whether coinage is to be used as a strategic commodity. To establish some sort of stable identity in an area, to encourage the idea among elites of some form of attachment to a group, an individual using coinage locally as a gift, can have the function of drawing peers together while demonstrating their equality and independence, thereby symbolically indicating that they have their own spaces, that areas are 'distant' from the minter. However, coinage which is used to develop strategic locations and encourage more experiences and opportunities among geographically long-distance elites can have the effect of shortening social distances, especially as coinage used in this way may well act as a symbol of a community of independent individuals – a polity led by an identified individual: the name on the coin. Currency in a province of the Roman Empire might be seen as 'abstract', distinct from individual interests and styles of life, and which gained significance through the purchase of goods. It would appear that later Iron Age coinage was much more tangible and gained its significance through the act of movement to engender experiences and opportunities from individuals/communities to other individuals/communities. However, while the coin's striker has jurisdiction over what it looks like and who gets it, it is up to the receiver as to how it is used and what for. This may well explain deposition at ritual sites.

To return to the Cherwell tribal boundary, it would be highly unlikely if Bagendon was producing coinage and the North Oxfordshire Grim's Ditch was not, and a much more compelling argument based on distribution of coinage would be that a late political entity developed across the watersheds of the Evenlode, Glyme and Cherwell, its influence being demonstrated by coin finds within its own limits and those further away. Coinage was also deposited on temple sites, not because they were at borders, but because they were connected with travel routes or on watersheds defining the self-imposed limits of that political entity. Those coins ending up in Hereford and Worcester, say, may well have been brought back to their source and deposited in temples as a token of thanksgiving for a successful journey. The lack of Western Series coins in areas to the south of the Grim's Ditch, the so-called 'core' areas, doesn't demonstrate that the *oppida* had nothing to do with the mechanics of wider trade-exchange routes, as it was only necessary to forge trade and social relationships with those up the line as an extension of 'incomer' trade.

The most recent attempt to use earthwork features as defining the tribal borders has been work on Aves Ditch, which has been considered among other possible roles as the boundary between the Catuvellauni and the Dobunni because of its proximity to the Cherwell (Sauer 2005). Such a boundary would be highly impermeable and in order to be maintained would need to policed in some way. One of the arguments for the identification of the earthwork as a border has been the Cherwell coin distribution discussed above and this no longer appears tenable. Equally, seeing the North Oxfordshire Grim's Ditch as part of that border, the evidence of an excursion of the Catuvellauni into Dobunnic territory as reported by Classical authors, and as a major territorial *oppida* without settlement in it, is also unlikely based on the evidence of the aerial photography of the mid-1990s. Even though the profile of the Aves Ditch and Grim's Ditch earthworks were similar at some points, their linear configurations are completely contrasting: sinuous versus straight, the second phase of the latter occurred after AD 43 rather than before it. There is, of course, the tempting issue of the straightness of the feature being the result of Roman pre-conquest influence on a tribal elite, which could be in line with the recent thinking of Creighton (2008). Looking at the earthwork from a later Iron Age perspective and not backwards from a Roman archaeologist's point of view, Aves Ditch could easily be interpreted as Roman and having a function connected to the soon to be established installation at Alchester, and the boundary theory might never have been presented. This will be discussed further in the next chapter.

Underlying the earthwork argument is that of the notion of tribal areas with centralised political power and very exact boundaries, in this case the Cherwell. In the case of Aves Ditch there is a considerable lack of settlement in the region to the east to ensure that such a boundary could be reinforced, and it also relegates those communities living on borders to being peripheral citizens who merely succumb to the whims and fancies of cultural ascription by larger and more powerful social forces, rather than being active agents who participate in an ongoing process of identity-construction themselves through interactions providing experiences and opportunities with both communities either side of a border.

Any discussion of a border between the two tribes would have to take into account the distinct lack of settlement of this date between the Alchester area and the Bierton/Aylesbury complex of sites. It is more likely that the early military establishment at Alchester was not about tribal borders and stopping aggression between the two entities, but about important trade routes already known to the Roman Army provincial leadership through occupied Gaul, having been trading along these routes for decades. Control of trade was a significant cause of the Roman Invasion.

perhaps a connection between Bierton and Alchester needed constructing. Beyond Alchester, the chronology becomes a bigger problem as there appears to be no direct relationship between the fort(ress) and the course of the road. The sharp turn to the west suggests that this was a new route and the dating evidence for this 'spur' is sparse and difficult to interpret. At Wilcote, Anthony Hands (1998) dated the construction of Akeman Street to AD 47, but that level of accuracy is hopelessly optimistic. The roadside settlement at Asthall has a mid first-century date (Booth 1997) but Akeman Street, when it approaches Cirencester, is seen as being a late addition (*c.* AD 70) to the road system (Hargreaves 1998). However, in an eventful two decades, it might not be surprising if sites were constructed, or developed, at different dates, as the established or changing identities of the communal groups responded differentially to the cultural contribution of the Romans.

VERLAMION/VERULAMIUM

It has long been argued that Roman towns were preceded by forts and their *vici* and that this was the case with both Verulamium and Corinium at the beginning and end of the journey along early Roman Akeman Street. The identification of a fort at Verulamium is based on the limited excavation of a rampart (Frere 1983) and possible gate beneath the later Insula XVII of the Roman town. However, the rampart was irregular in line and the plan of the gate, which became known as the 'Timber Tower', is not easily related to more standard forts of the period. Evidence for internal buildings, such as barrack blocks, was absent and the few military items from the town which include two *loricae*, a complete helmet (Niblett 2001) and a range of other military equipment, correspond with the incidence of those found on other sites in Roman Britain (Haselgrove and Millet 1997). Creighton (2006) has argued that items of military equipment were possibly pre-conquest, the result of sons of the elite returning from attachments to military units in Gaul or other parts of the Empire and using them as ritual offerings on a safe return, and Niblett suggests a similar trend, but in the context of the post-conquest period when British veterans returned from service with auxiliary regiments in other parts of the Empire. The presence of Roman military accoutrements need not indicate the presence of the Roman Army, as owning such fittings may also suggest a need for display by pre-conquest elites.

Another of Frere's arguments was that the course of Watling Street cut diagonally across the later town grid which would position a fort somewhere between the river and the later forum and basilica complex which is where the 'rampart' and 'gate' were discovered. However, between 1986 and 1988 excavations south of the forum demonstrated that even in its earliest form, Watling Street had never cut diagonally across the central part of the town, but was constructed in the AD 70-80 period and was focused on the then Roman town. Any previous north–south route may well have been behind the Prae Wood embankments. The evidence taken as a whole indicates that it is difficult to sustain the conclusion that a fort, occupied for about six years up until AD 49, existed. Haselgrove and Millett (1977, 294-5) suggest two further options:

i) Since the area was arguably pro-Roman, and therefore there was no need to quell local resistance, any fort underneath the town would have been of short duration, a matter of months rather than years, and not to oversee the native community, but simply a temporarily occupied camp in an already conquered and friendly territory.
ii) The rampart and gate might be interpreted as entirely 'native' in its construction and function, demarcating the margins of the expanding settlement in the early years of the conquest.

Either interpretation removes the role of the army in the development of the town, the gateway being seen as the piles of the original road across the river on the north-east side of the town. Indeed, Reece (1985, 15-16) has commented that there are too few Claudian coins compared with other military sites to suggest a sustained military occupation. Equally, these arguments indicate that there would be no need for a fort in a pro-Roman friendly area and can be applied equally to either a proposed site above the town to the south-west at Windridge Farm or Kingsbury, though both sites look attractive in the former's position above and just south of Akeman Street and with the latter overlooking the Ver crossing. If either existed, they may have been a short-term response to the revolt of Boudicca, which in turn may suggest that the local population might also have taken a part in that insurrection which could have been more widespread than the Roman sources were prepared to admit.

An important factor in the discussion of pre-Flavian Verulamium is the context of the Folly Lane burial (Niblett 1990). Clearly after AD 43, perhaps as late as AD 60, it indicates, in some aspects at least, a later Iron Age lifestyle was continuing – the rites carried out there are very much in a late Iron Age style, but clearly the aristocratic tradition now involved the wearing of Roman armour, and a taste for Roman lifestyle. How much of this identity change was due to the experience of the aristocrat buried there personally travelling to other parts of the Roman Empire, or to the mobility of goods, the Romans 'selling' their culture, cannot be known. However, the distinctive Folly Lane burial was to be an important event in the life of Roman Verulamium throughout its existence as it determined the layout and expansion of the settlement and demonstrated that it was a significant site of memory. Its position on the skyline immediately marks it out as of great consequence, and that the Roman administration allowed such a potent symbol of power and identity to be so visible in such an important culturally geographical position indicates an agreement of some sort with the local population. That visibility was clearly a high-status indicator is evident in the Prae Wood structures being 'concealed' behind a linear bank. It is likely also that the Folly Lane site was important before the aristocratic burial in the presence of a shrine also behind a bank, in which case the burial would have been an even more potent act indicating continuity with the past. This might also suggest that the pre-Flavian settlement was already growing with its main street aligned on an earlier ritual site which was re-emphasised by the Folly Lane burial.

By AD 61, Roman Verulamium only covered a small area around what was to become the forum/basilica complex, the rapidly expanding settlement had spread across the central enclosure and annexe. A few streets in the central area were probably already in place, although they did not necessarily extend far, and they were only lightly metalled un-cambered tracks. Remains of buildings are also rare; traces of some timber-framed structures and a workshop have been found. Masonry buildings were also beginning to appear, along with an expensively and elaborately decorated bath house, and the 'proto' forum may also date from this period. The local elites were losing no time in allying themselves with the prevailing new system of governance with its imported culture, and, as a result, Verulamium was already developing into a fully Romanised town, that is until the events of AD 61 when the Boudiccan Revolt caused a setback. The Folly Lane burial itself may have been a memorial to what had already been completed, and the layout of the early town might have been the achievement of the person buried there, the alignment of the road out of the town to the east already focused on a shrine already on the hillside. Gorhambury continued to develop with the circular building being replaced by a fairly large building constructed soon after the conquest. The rectangular-based structure comprised of a suite of three rooms running north–south with at least one wing room which was destroyed in the Boudiccan rebellion. The shrine at Wood End Lane seems to have continued in its earlier form.

NORTHCHURCH

Along the Bulbourne valley the industrial activity continued uninterrupted. There is a very limited amount of evidence for the Roman Army in terms of a skillet handle, an unusual belt mount of some opposing acorns and a hinge from *lorica segmentata*, but this is highly superficial and might have been the result of a number of processes that were not directly military. However, it is possible that there was some sort of army presence to oversee an important area of iron-working which would have been of great significance in supplying the Roman Army with a source of metal for the manufacture of armour, weapons etc. This might emphasise a link to the fort(ress) at Alchester and not necessarily part of a military controlled zone, which would seem out of place considering the developments in Verulamium.

FLEET MARSDEN

Fleet Marsden has been suggested as a fort site largely because of the later small town that grew up in that location at a later period and which covered up to 45 acres, but it may have begun its life in an earlier roadside settlement role. There is no reliable evidence of a military base here even though it is halfway between Northchurch and Alchester.

ALCHESTER

Without doubt, the discovery of a military base at Alchester is one of the most significant events of recent Roman archaeological studies and is also important in its implications for our understanding of the later Iron Age (Sauer 2000). Fieldwalking and metal detectorist activity had indicated that there had been mid first-century military activity in the area, and this was confirmed by the analysis of aerial photographs followed by further fieldwork and excavation (*19*). The aerial photographs showed a marching camp, a parade ground and a Roman fort. In retrospect the rather strange bow-shaped course of Akeman Street which pivoted at this point should have indicated that there was something of strategic importance in the area even though any obvious site would have easily been water-logged and in the 'defence' shadow of Arncott Hill, itself suggesting that there was no potential for an attack from the east. Any traveller would have been impressed by exotic rectangular wooden walls and towers, and even if they had seen structures with right-angled corners at Verulamium, they were not of this scale. However, it is very hard for rectangular structures to appear 'organic' and dynamic and this, as well as the daily, fixed round of the soldiers' activities, may well have alerted the traveller to the 'Other'.

The most important aspect of the discovery of this military complex is its gate posts which have been dated by dendrochronology to late AD 44 or early AD 45, within a year of the Invasion events. However, it remains uncertain exactly what form this military establishment took, or whether it is only of one phase: 44 AD to the late 50s or early 60s. No doubt some of these problems will be solved with the full publication of the recent investigations.

This military installation has been the subject of limited excavation, substantially less than one per cent (Sauer 2006, 17) of the site has been explored. Most of this has been done through trenching in order to discover the extent of the installation and therefore has not given the breadth of information that selective open-area excavation might; the problems of effectively sampling through the site are clear. A 'probable' *fabricam* in 2003 became a *principia*, and in 2004 'barracks'. The position of the defences of the 'main fortress' keep shifting south and a set of two military granaries (one rebuilt) are postulated on the evidence of two trenches.

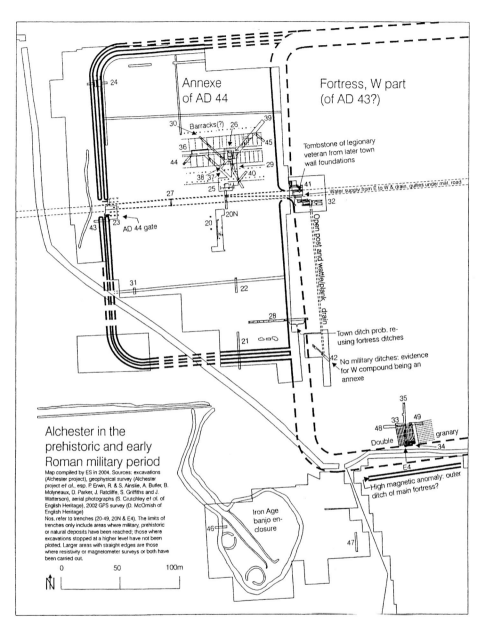

Annexe
of AD 44

Fortress, W part
(of AD 43?)

Barracks(?)

Tombstone of legionary
veteran from later town
wall foundations

Water supply from E to W & drain gullies under milt. road

Open post and wattle/plank drain

AD 44 gate

Town ditch prob. re-
using fortress ditches

No military ditches: evidence
for W compound being an
annexe

granary

Double

High magnetic anomaly: outer
ditch of main fortress?

Alchester in the prehistoric and early Roman military period

Map compiled by ES in 2004. Sources: excavations
(Alchester project), geophysical survey (Alchester
project *et al.*, esp. P. Erwin, R. & S. Ainslie, A. Butler, B.
Molyneaux, D. Parker, J. Ratcliffe, S. Griffiths and J.
Watterson), aerial photographs (S. Crutchley *et al.* of
English Heritage), 2002 GPS survey (D. McOmish of
English Heritage)
Nos. refer to trenches (20-49, 20N & E4). The limits of
trenches only include areas where military, prehistoric
or natural deposits have been reached; those where
excavations stopped at a higher level have not been
plotted. Larger areas with straight edges are those
where resistivity or magnetometer surveys or both have
been carried out.

0   50   100m

Iron Age
banjo en-
closure

19 Alchester in the prehistoric and early Roman period (after Sauer 2005)

While there is no doubt that an early military installation did exist at Alchester, its identification as a vexillation fortress, the nature of the later Iron Age settlement surrounding it and the speculative considerations of the type of garrison and the role of the installation in the conquest of Britannia rather detract from the value of the interpretations of the site. The discovery of fragments of an early tombstone retrieved from the later town wall indicate that a veteran of the Second Augustan Legion, Lucius Valerius Geminus was buried in the area. Consideration of the rarity of veterans being buried away from the fortress of the legions in which they served adds importance to this find which might indicate the presence of at least part of that legion being at Alchester. However, to suggest that 'Alchester was in all probability the base established and occupied for several winters by one of the most famous persons in ancient history, Vespasian' is highly speculative (Sauer 2005b, 93). However, this should not detract from the enthusiasm and commitment of Sauer in the discovery and exploration of this fascinating and significant early Roman site.

It is still unclear at the time of writing whether there is merely one compound, dendro-dated to AD 44 or whether this is an annexe to a larger early compound – of AD 43 perhaps. In the former case we are probably dealing with a fortress of roughly 8ha in size, in the latter with a main fortress of 12-13ha plus an annexe of *c*.4ha. However, the excavator admits that while it seems most likely that the latter theory is correct, there is still no definite evidence for a decision one way or another. Clearly, the dendro-date of late AD 44 or early AD 45 is important not only for the installation, but studies of Roman Britain as a whole; however, dating evidence for the withdrawal of the military garrison from Alchester is uncertain, the excavator signifying the late AD 50s or the beginning of the AD 60s, at the latest.

Sauer has suggested that the Alchester 'fortress' lay at a point where the westward route from the Colchester fortress and the northern route from the Chichester fortress met. Therefore the garrison was in an ideal position to control the recently annexed territories and the supply routes at the key road junction which strongly suggests, at the very least, a fortress; such sophisticated defences and permanent wooden buildings would also indicate that it was never intended to be a transient installation. Sauer has made valid points about the siting of the military establishment in a position to control routes. The route from the north-west to south-east and north to south made this location probably one of the most important in Britannia. It will be argued below that the road from Verulamium stopped at Alchester with the continued use of bog-iron from the Bulbourne valley being essential for the army. The unusual aspect of this case it that Alchester was not backed up by a string of forts from Verulamium and there was only a possible fort at Dorchester to the south which could have been connected with it, though as far as we know at present the Dorchester fort, the existence of which is based on very limited evidence, was not in existence until the AD 60s, and perhaps also a response to the Boudiccan rebellion. The other rather strange circumstance is the physical position of the fort(ress). In an area which was known for its high water table (and which has preserved evidence for the site so well) the structures are not well sited nor is the position in the 'defence shadow' of a prominent high ground, Graven Hill, easily explained. Presumably, Graven Hill was a significant marker in the landscape and as such the fort(ress) could have been a considerable statement about new ownership of that landscape. Certainly, the fort(ress) has no obvious relationship with Akeman Street which is either later or earlier than the military site. There is also drier ground close by which would have enabled exactly the same function to be undertaken. The problem is not one that can be solved by archaeology, although there is some evidence of high-status later Iron Age structures close by to the north (Booth *et al.* 2001). The variety of military structures at Alchester probably indicates a range of dates and functions over a long period, where the only relative chronology between the structures is the parade ground reusing a ditch from the marching camp and therefore post-dating it. The marching camp might be seen as part of a policing policy after the more permanent (and first?) military establishment has been abandoned, or a staging post for troops moving up to the frontier. The presence of a later military post on the crossroads has been raised by Booth. The chronology of the establishment needs to be further refined as if the fortress was occupied until the AD 60s, it has to be explained why it was needed when sites such as Verulamium and Corinium were beginning to grow and surely the frontier, if that is what the fort(ress) was part of, had moved further north. Perhaps the publication of the definitive report of the excavations and further work might indicate that there were several occupations of the site by the military, or that it survived as a supply base supporting the army further north and west.

AVES DITCH

Aves Ditch with its 4.2km virtually straight course is clearly a surveyed earthwork aligned south–west to north–east and seemingly delineating part of the Cherwell valley. It was discussed in the previous chapter because the excavator considered it to be of a later Iron Age origin. Our present knowledge of it derives from six cross-sectional trenches and a water pipeline which transects all excavated on the straight section between the Gorse and the monument's south–western extremity. Sauer (2005a) has published the results of six of these trenches, three of which were dug in 1937 by Captain Christopher Musgrave and the rest 60 years later, both campaigns being undertaken by the Oxford University Archaeological Society. The pipeline transect was undertaken by Cotswold Archaeology in 2004–5 who retrieved no dating evidence.

Aves Ditch has variously been interpreted as either a road or a linear earthwork, but Sauer's report has demonstrated a bank with a ditch which was cut through hard limestone, and to the west of it, thereby facing into the plateau area. The sections recorded in both excavations indicate that the ditch was between 1.5m and 2m deep, therefore suggesting a bank of the same dimensions. The ditch appears to have filled naturally with no evidence of re-cutting evident in the water pipeline section. No traces of timber framework on the bank's crest or palisade on the outer lip of the ditch could be detected as a result of the narrowness of trench. Sauer set up a discussion on the construction of the earthwork: if it was an early Roman military earthwork or a road, then entrenchment tools of similar quality to our modern tools would probably have been in plentiful supply; if it dates back to the later Iron Age then the question of equipment used is more problematic. Suitable iron tools such as picks and adzes had already become available well before the conquest, but in the light of their comparative scarcity, it was not necessary to presume that Aves Ditch was excavated by a team equipped with iron tools. Sauer also hypothesises that 100 people working 215-360 eight-hour days would be necessary for the 4.2m of bank and ditch to be constructed, and he admits that a team equipped with iron tools, especially if consisting of trained Roman soldiers, would have been somewhat faster.

The 1937 campaign, which was not particularly well recorded, resulted in a published date in the Roman period derived mainly from pottery. However, radiocarbon and archaeomagnetic dates from the most recent interventions indicate a range of 500 BC to AD 550, though not a single Roman or post-Roman sherd or other object was found embedded in the bank or even bottom silt of the ditch of the linear feature. Much of the pottery from the 1937 excavations, though then identified as Roman, has now been considered the result of mis-attribution. The excavator also suggests that some of the later Iron Age finds could in theory still have been discarded within a generation after the conquest of AD 43, while no diagnostic Roman objects need have been lost within the first few months of Roman rule and that the absence of Roman material from the bank or ditch argues, in any case, against a construction date several decades after the Roman Invasion. The incidence of any finds being discovered in three such narrow sections along such an extensive earthwork is very low, and with possible Iron Age settlement in the immediate area the problems of residual pottery in the soil can be a problem.

It is difficult to ignore the position of the very early military establishment so close at Alchester in regard to this straight section of bank and ditch in a relatively thinly populated area in the later Iron Age, especially as much of the evidence for structures of that date lay west of the earthwork. The last chapter suggested that there was little evidence for a border in the region in the later Iron Age, and also a lack of settlement around the Alchester area, so it might be safer to use the later dates of Sauer's spectrum and to see the feature as early Roman, either in date or influence, and closely connected to the position of the Alchester military sites. Such an earthwork need not be directly concerned with settlement but with controlling and overseeing mobility and movement of people and goods thereby providing a control, not only on the Portway to the south, but also to the north-west to south-east routes, and after the construction of Akeman Street, from the west to east. The straightness of Aves Ditch surely suggests a Roman origin, and while this can be argued as being the result of a strong later Iron Age aristocracy-led drive to imitate elements of Roman culture, including, occasionally, rectilinear architecture, it could have been made redundant very quickly with the establishment of the fort(ress) adjacent. There needs to be further research and more sections through the monument to add to the two recently completed full sections and give further dating, though the loss of artefacts along the length of the route may not be detected in single narrow trenches.

It is likely that the answer to the function of the earthwork lies in the wider landscape. Aves Ditch may always be a problem, especially with the possibilities of residual pottery, and given the discovery of the beheaded Saxon burial in one of Sauer's trenches and the importance of the Bicester area as a border stronghold in that period, there is no reason why it might not of have been of that date, though its value as a defensive or boundary indicator is subject to the same provisos as for a later Iron Age or Roman origin. Most likely on present evidence it was reused at that time. For whatever the reason it was built, it must have been in relation to another feature to give it a substantial role, otherwise it is just an anomalous stretch of earthwork that had so little obvious purpose. It is of a totally different character to the North Oxfordshire Grim's Ditch and is therefore more likely to have related to the Alchester site. Whatever its purpose it would have remained a fascinating feature in the landscape drawing to it interesting creation myths.

SANSOM'S PLATT

There is some evidence for the continuation of this settlement after the later Iron Age into the early Roman period as a possible religious site and a potential market, although this evidence is only from fieldwalking. Aerial photography has demonstrated that it became significantly more important at a later date. Closely related to Sansom's Platt, but on the western side of the Glyme, is a settlement which may well have been an early small town discovered by fieldwalking for the Woodstock bypass. While such a settlement might be seen as serving the needs of travellers, its position just outside the Grim's Ditch Phase Two might be seen as significant considering the absence of roadside settlement inside the earthwork boundaries. However, a more complete discussion is undertaken below.

NORTH OXFORDSHIRE GRIM'S DITCH PHASE TWO

Some time after the line of Akeman Street was established, probably after the mid to late 40s AD, Phase Two of the North Oxfordshire Grim's Ditch was constructed to enclose an area of almost 80 sq km with sections of discontinuous earthworks (*20*).

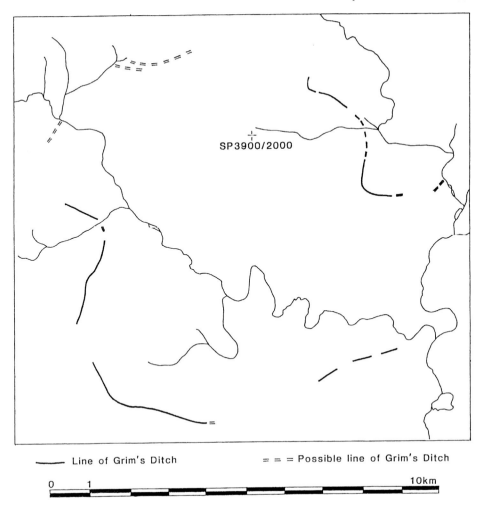

SP 3900/2000

━━━ Line of Grim's Ditch   = = = Possible line of Grim's Ditch

0   1   10km

20 The North Oxfordshire Grim's Ditch Phase Two

Two stratigraphical relationships are important in making this claim. The first is the cutting of the Phase One and Two earthworks in the Ditchley area where it appears that the larger of the phases is later than the Phase One as described in the previous chapter, though the time lag between their construction is impossible to ascertain with present evidence, but appears to have been short due to the amount of silt in the ditch bottom before it was deliberately partially back-filled. Second is the interpretation of the relationship of the Phase Two earthwork with Akeman Street in Blenheim Park. Haverfield's excavations in 1898 seemingly demonstrated that the road cut through the banks of the Phase Two earthwork at that point, making the road later than the bank, although further detail is lacking as his work was only published in note form. However, Crawford in his paper published in *Antiquity* in 1930 rather disparagingly dismissed Haverfield's results out of hand – Haverfield's excavations were 'inconclusive and had better be forgotten'. Crawford's main argument was that the sharp bend of the 'hook' in the earthwork's course above the Glyme 'strongly suggests that the Roman road was already in position there when the ditch was made'. Crawford was defending his late Roman theory for the date of the Ditch based on its protecting the density of late villas within the area from Saxon incursion. Excavations along the line of the Blenheim section of the Phase Two earthwork (Harden 1937) identified 'butt-ends' either side of the Akeman Street route, but came to the conclusion that Akeman Street must have been following an Iron Age precursor. It is much simpler to accept that it would be unlikely for a Roman road to aim for a narrow pre-existing gap and that the evidence of the surveyed course indicates that it was designed as a long-distance route and not with just local considerations influencing its course. The evidence of the 'hook' of the earthwork above the Glyme demonstrates that the earthwork is respecting the Roman road and could also have been intended to make north–south traffic following the western bank of the river be routed along the eastern bank, thereby excluding movement into the Grim's Ditch area.

There is no political problem with this later phase of the earthworks being constructed up to the road. The bank and ditch, and possible palisade trench, as in Phase One, would have been no threat to the army and it would in many ways formalise a relationship between the two groups that had probably been in existence for some time. That the Phase Two of the North Oxfordshire Grim's Ditch has its axis on Akeman Street indicates that it was an entirely different conception than the *oppida* of Phase One. The consequences of this are that the area enclosed by the circuit of earthworks of Phase Two forms the largest enclosure of landscape at any period within the British Isles and this gives some idea of its potential in terms of power relationships and trade. As the earthworks of both phases have a similar profile and the Phase One earthworks were not completely slighted, and the bank and ditch still recognisable in the landscape, we can detect a continuity of a social grouping and respect for the ritual functions from an earlier period – a sign of continuity of memory and identity. That the Phase Two earthwork was discontinuous might indicate there was no reason for the earthworks to have an uninterrupted linear boundary as in Phase One, as the function of the space enclosed was different. If this was the case then it would be possible to use woods as part of the limits of ownership as there would have been agreed boundaries. Within the Phase Two circuit the confluence of the Glyme and Evenlode appear to have had a special import and this may well be one of waterborne trade to the Thames.

What is highly significant about Phase Two of the Grim's Ditch earthwork is that it encloses all the already identified major later Iron Age settlements between the Glyme and Windrush which were to be the sites of the early villas of the next chapter and this indicates a measure of continuity not only of settlement but of social cohesion. Whatever was special about this area between the Glyme and Windrush, it was to remain influential throughout the rest of the Roman period, even when the ditch of the Phase Two earthworks was allowed to silt up naturally and with no recutting or replacement of the palisade (Copeland 1988).

Akeman Street takes up a new alignment to ensure a direct crossing of the Evenlode at the Stonesfield ford otherwise it would have gone too far to the north and encountered some very steep slopes in the area now under Wychwood Forest. As a result of this, or because of it, the road passes to the south of the North Oxfordshire Grim's Ditch Phase One. Akeman Street climbs gradually up from the Evenlode to a point about 5km from the river when the view begins to open out to the north-east, with the plateau beyond the Evenlode in view and then higher up near Wilcote the whole of the area within the Phase Two enclosure can be seen making it a very significant locality.

WILCOTE

Although a large number of Claudian coins were found near the Wilcote settlement, these need not necessarily be related to an army presence. However, the evidence for a large number of stone quarries along the road indicates that in the years immediately after the building of Akeman Street, they provided road surfacing from the Oolitic limestone rubble worn out of the rock outcrops in the area. All the structures located by the excavator, Anthony Hands, were simple and of timber and post hole construction and appear to be a road builders' camp, perhaps supervised by the military. Since there is no evidence of a later Iron Age presence the settlement must have been purpose-built (Hands 1998). Whether it had a service role in terms of the army's need for staging posts at regular intervals is doubtful considering the existence of Samson's Platt and Asthall. It is also possible that the army would not have put this type of post within the larger Grim's Ditch enclosure considering the perceived importance of the area.

Above Wilcote, a bank about one metre high appears in the present landscape, which is the other side of Phase Two of the Grim's Ditch and at which point Akeman Street passes. The Roman road moves west, gradually losing height until the valley of the Windrush is crossed, possible traces of the bridge abutments still being visible.

ASTHALL

A marching camp of 0.85ha, an undated temporary fortification for troops, located on the south side of Akeman Street and aligned to it, was identified by aerial photography (Welfare and Swann 1994). The alignment of the camp leaves no doubt about the importance of the road at an early date and suggests that Akeman Street had been laid out if not surfaced by then (*21*). However, there is no need to think of this presence as in any way permanent, as there must have

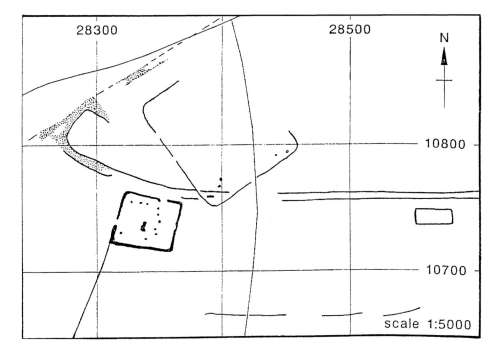

21 Roman temporary camp at Asthall (Oxford Archaeology)

been troops travelling through friendly areas on their way to other destinations where the military action was taking place. There has been speculation about a more permanent fort in the area based on its position where Akeman Street crosses the Windrush, and a find of a *gladius* handle and pottery of an early date have been used to support this. However, the evidence is very limited and not persuasive, and the artefacts could equally have originated in the temporary camp which could have had a role in the construction of the road (Booth 1997). The non-military evidence suggests a mid first-century date for the civilian settlement, demonstrating the beginnings of commercial movement or a market town for the immediate locality. With little Iron Age settlement in the area, or on the road's course to the Bagendon/Cirencester area, it is unlikely that there needed to be a fort in this location as the sheltered site of Asthall sits in an abandoned meander core. Sites further astride Akeman Street at Coln St Aldwyns and Quenington, 16km south-west of Asthall, are likely to be later in the second century (RCHME 1976).

THE WELSH WAY

If it can be presumed that the major axis of trade remained north-west to south-east and therefore the Welsh Way retained its importance as a major communication route, the building of Akeman Street from the North Oxfordshire Grim's Ditch to the Bagendon/Cirencester area may have been undertaken for political as well as military or trade reasons. Since the Akeman Street approach to Cirencester is demonstrably later, possibly in the AD 70s, it is likely that the early Roman route followed the course of the Welsh Way through Bagendon and up to Ermine Street. Field enclosures in the nineteenth century have altered the route giving it right-angled bends at times. However, over the course of the Welsh Way from Barnsley to Bagendon, there is a straightness that might be the result of the surveying and straightening of an older route which would imply control by the Roman army. As will be seen below, Akeman Street appears to have had no relationship with the proposed early fort at Cirencester which seems to have its axis on Ermine Street, and no relationship with the White Way. The Barnsley site remains very problematic in that it has not produced evidence of this date (although some of the Roman pottery might be dated earlier).

THE BAGENDON COMPLEX

The Ditches site appears to have been continually occupied in this period, with the infilling of the enclosure ditch and creation of the causeway across the ditch, but the areas where there is most likely to be evidence relating to this period have not yet been excavated (Trow *et al.* forthcoming). It would appear that the activity at Bagendon ceased around the AD 60s after a short period of intense activity. Richard Reece (1990) has suggested that the settlement behind the dykes looks less like a Belgic *oppidum* and more like an early Roman industrial centre and it was this production role that was different in quality from the high-status settlement at Ditches. The settlement immediately behind the dykes occupies a very small area and it does not seem to be of great intensity or complexity, with very little evidence of people living there in any number. No feature from either of the excavations undertaken there suggests a town or proto-town. The presence of a high-status building underneath the present village may be a possibility. The Duntisbournes may have been abandoned though it is feasible that they share the same chronology as the Bagendon settlement.

The continuous use of the Welsh Way could have been the reason for the dykes and it was only when the route fell out of use, probably because of the construction of Akeman Street, that the settlement failed. With the growth of Corinium, either as a new site or on the site of a previous settlement, Bagendon would not have survived, but the Welsh Way might still have served as a routeway from the Thames valley for goods not carried on the main surfaced roads. The whole notion of Bagendon being an *oppidum* whose population moved to Corinium is becoming increasingly insupportable in the light of evidence from behind the dykes and the general lack of settlement in the immediate landscape.

ERMINE STREET

In the mid AD 50s, at the same point above the valley of the Bagendon Brook at which the journey of the previous chapter ended, travellers would have stood alongside what would have certainly been Ermine Street. This metalled road supplied the fortress of Kingsholm, in a meander of the River Severn at it lowest crossing point and strategically important in the continued military activity to obtain the land of the Silures in South Wales, as well as the iron and coal from the Forest of Dean. If travellers had turned south on the recently surveyed and metalled Ermine Street, though almost certainly on an older route, they would be travelling to Silchester through what was to become Corinium at Cirencester.

CORINIUM

There is conflicting evidence for the exact status of any settlement at Cirencester in the early Roman years and specifically for the presence of a military base and the function it would have played. The discovery of the tombstones of two troopers from cavalry regiments, Dannicus a tribesman of the Raurici whose chief town was Augusta Raurici the modern Augst, near Basel in Switzerland, and Sextus Valerius Genialis, a trooper of the ala Thracum, are certain evidence of a military presence somewhere in the area and this has in turn been extended to suggest two periods of occupation for a putative fort. The problem lies in the archaeological evidence for the Leaholme fort's design and garrison, as excavations in 1961, 1964, 1974 and 1980 have provided somewhat conflicting evidence for such a military base (McWhirr 1981). A pair of parallel very unsubstantial ditches were discovered, being 0.65m wide and 1.25m deep, forming a very unusual configuration for those of a fort (*22*). Geophysical survey has provided inconclusive results about the course of the ditches on other sides of the proposed military base. The dimension of the ditches might be explained away by a high water table making it unnecessary for any deeper features, as the shallow ones would form a moat. Analysing this evidence led the excavators to suggest that they represented a *hibernia* (winter quarters) associated with the early years of the Invasion and early military contact. This activity has been dated *c.*AD 50/55, but its duration is problematic and if there was a military presence it was a passing one of no more than six months, possibly founded to reassure a Dobunnic hierarchy at Bagendon during the early phase of the Welsh campaign which may have produced unsettled conditions in the Cotswold area. Such a fort might have been sited to act as a reserve base for the fortress at Kingsholm, or as a continually changing garrison with troops moving through to the then fighting front of the Welsh campaign. This might explain the tombstones of troopers from two different regiments. The date of the second phase of the defensive circuit of the Leaholme fort has been proposed as *c.*AD 65/70 although it might have been earlier and a response

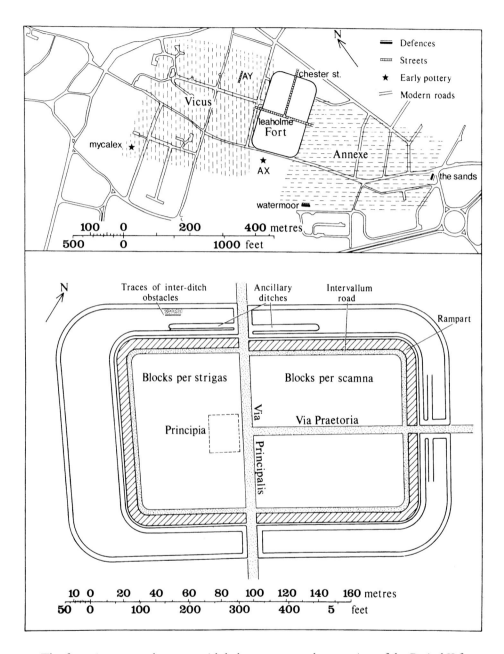

22 The fort, *vicus* area and annexe with below a suggested restoration of the Period II fort. (Cirencester Excavation Committee)

to the news of the Boudiccan rebellion travelling quickly along Akeman Street and causing anxiety among pro-Roman groups. Again, this could offer another opportunity for the two regiments to be stationed in the fort.

Internal buildings of the proposed military base have been located which were of timber, both individual posts and post-in-trench, possibly constructed in three phases, but sufficient plans for the function of the buildings to be deduced have not been recovered. What needs to be explained is the type of garrison which might undertake a substantial role yet fit into a fort of just 1.8ha (4.5 acres). Certainly 500 men in a cavalry regiment and with the need for stables would have had problems with that amount of space. There is very little evidence for a fort on the proposed site, and what there is has been subject to many caveats, for example that there was no timber lacing in the rampart of the second fort (which would be expected), or that none of the small finds recovered from this site help with the dating of the rampart or has any particular military associations. Reece has also commented that the number of coins recovered indicates a very short and passing military presence on the site.

Among the positive arguments for a fort on this particular site is the pottery which clearly is of the same fabrics and manufacture as that from the fortress at Kingsholm which was not abandoned until AD 60. Such pottery styles have also been discovered at Silchester and it is likely that we are looking at the movement of soldiers up to the frontier from the south. A large deposit of ceramic material in the Leaholme fort ditches indicates the abandonment of the base rather than a change of garrison. Samian vessels from the ditch had clearly never been used and some were types not likely to have been in demand by soldiers and a late date for the types could be because they were discarded direct from a store for disposal in the ditch, and had never been issued, all of which confuses discussion of the function of the structures even more. There are interesting parallels with the problems of a fort at Verulamium, and the relationship of the central enclosure to a marshy area with a high water table. When the ditch of the southern arm of the central enclosure was levelled in *c.*AD 70, large quantities of fine wares and samian were dumped in it. What might be of significance is the relationship of the fort to the Roman roads around it. The Leaholme fort would have been laid out on the axis of Ermine Street and have had no direct relationship with either the Fosse Way or any early form of Akeman Street.

THE MILITARY TRAVELLER IMPOSING CHANGE?

Identifying the variety of functions of an early Akeman Street in response to the varied 'maturity' of communities along it and their relationships to the establishment of a Roman province encapsulates many of the current debates about the creation of the province of Britannia – those of a sharp break between the later Iron Age societies in AD 43, a 'conquest' or 'invasion' of southern England, or an annexation of a region already under *de facto* Roman rule. Also highlighted in these contentious issues is the veracity of the sources used. The reports of Classical writers, Tacitus and Dio Cassius for example, are seen as being accurate sources for the events of the early period, however, the long discussions which have been undertaken about where the Roman Army landed demonstrate the difficulty of interpreting these sources, and also the overwhelming focus on the Roman Army to the detriment of the later Iron Age societies and the landscapes into which the Roman army moved. The prevailing impression it is that Classical historical archaeology is driving the research process with the later Iron Age archaeology only being acknowledged if it agrees with these problematic sources.

While Davies (2004) suggested that Akeman Street was 'territory holding road', Ainslie (2005) considered the possibility of the road being a section of very early *limes*. The *limes* proposal is argued from the point of view of forts along Akeman Street being a day's march apart, joining the early fortress at Colchester or the small settlement of London with Cirencester and then via the Fosse Way to a vexillation fortress at Lake Farm near Poole in Dorset, occupied by the Second Augustan Legion, part of which Sauer proposes as the garrison of Alchester under the leadership of Vespasian. The *limes* schema is attractive geographically, particularly as the bow-shaped course of Akeman Street appears to be facing outwards into anti-Roman areas, providing a longer perimeter than a straight road which invites its interpretation as 'stop-line', not necessarily for the movement of troops quickly. Large parts of the *limes* conception are derived from a hypothesis that 'it is possible to reconstruct a network of forts with a fair degree of plausibility' (Webster 1980, 22). These proposed military establishments on the line of Akeman Street (his route 26), were at St Albans (fort known), Northchurch (possible fort site with some evidence), near Fleet Marsden (postulated site with no evidence), Alchester (postulated fort site with some evidence), Asthall (possible fort site near a later settlement), and Cirencester (fort known). As we have seen, it is highly unlikely that there was a military establishment at Verulamium, and substantial evidence for Northchurch and Fleet Marsden is lacking. Similarly, there is only evidence for a marching camp at Asthall, and at Cirencester the early fort seems more related to Ermine Street than Akeman Street. Behind the Akeman Street line a fort has been proposed at Dorchester on *apriori* terms, but the only evidence is from a post-Boudiccan period when the occupation of the second short-lived fort was probably constructed at Cirencester. It has also been suggested (Booth 1977) that one of the phases of military occupation at Alchester might have been the result of the same impulse by the army after the rebellion of AD 61 as news travelled quickly down Akeman Street from Verulamium. Another variation on the *limes* concept is that the barrier was not to keep aggressive forces out from the north, but to ensure that it was the south that was conquered by preventing escape north, to contain the enemy. However, on the dating evidence presented here and the lack of the required forts, it seems that the *limes* concept is unlikely, particularly as the development of such a military strategy in the province of Britannia was not needed until the early second century with the construction of Hadrian's Wall.

So, what was the strategy behind a military base in the South Midlands barely a year after the AD 43 Invasion? Sauer has seen the fort in the territory of the West Catuvellauni as 'Rome was here confronted with much more powerful enemies' (2000, 21) and more specifically to stop any attacks by the Catuvellauni on the Dobunni. Perhaps this is over-stating the issue. There does not seem to be evidence of any considerable later Iron Age settlement in the area of Alchester, except for a possible banjo enclosure near the marching camp, and the earthworks of the North Oxfordshire Grim's Ditch. The concept of unified tribal blocks has also been seen to be unsafe before the Roman conquest and possibly for some time after it. So, the only secure evidence for a military role for Akeman Street is from the establishment at Alchester, which seems to have had no clear relationship with the early Akeman Street. There is even a problem about exactly what sort of military base produced the gatepost dendrochronological date of AD 44-5. Was it a fort or fortress? While it is clear that Alchester is certainly a military site, it is not clear whether it was a fort or a vexillation fortress, and this is made more difficult by the inter-changeability of the terms in the *Archaeological Journal* paper of 2000. In the summary of his work at Alchester (2007, 29), Sauer has made valuable proposals for the future, drawing our attention to the perilous state of the site with the lowering of the water table which protects its wooden structures. However, he admits that there is a need for further fieldwork to demonstrate the hypothesis of the postulated fortress and to search for evidence of this postulated feature's date of construction.

With the evidence for a vexillation fortress being problematic, it might be better to propose a fort to control/monitor the crucial trade routes to the south and south-east from the Midlands and the central Welsh border – a man-made contribution to the cultural geography of the area – specifically the Cherwell route. The evidence of the double granaries, if indeed that is what they were, might be considered to be later than the fort and part of a supply base set up to ensure that the army moving into the Midlands was not short of food and equipment. The re-occupation of the site in a post-Boudiccan scenario could have been to protect a supply base or to safeguard an important route to the south coast. If Akeman Street as a *limes* did exist perhaps we should we be looking at the period immediately after AD 61.

SETTLERS AND 'ROMAN INVASION'

Haselgrove and Millet (1997) proposed a continuation of a pre-existing later Iron Age social system for at least a decade after AD 43 in specific localities. Each of the *oppida* along Roman Akeman Street has evidence of a continuing identity well after AD 43. Verulamium has the continuation of the central enclosure and more significant perhaps the Folly Lane burial which determined the layout of the settlement throughout the Roman period. It may also have been the event that allowed the Roman administration to consider that it was time to actively involve themselves in the development of the town, because it was seen as an end of an era for that part of the Catuvallauni which had supported the Romans by changing their own political status. The Grim's Ditch seems to have been extended with the building of Phase Two aligned on the new Roman road of Akeman Street and Bagendon appears to have continued as a trading settlement again until the AD 60s, and surely the Welsh Way survived throughout the Roman period. This suggests that allowing established movements within the landscape to continue without interruption may well have been a continuation of trade routes that the Romans had actively supported before AD 43. The acceptance of these entities as locations of power, identity and memory by the Romans indicates that rather than imposing Roman ways of life on the elites they would encourage the change in identities through internal motivations, and with the increase in trade this change in identities may well have occurred, through movement and mobility, along the whole length of the Romanised route we know as Akeman Street.

The process of change was double-faceted. One of the major influences on the Invasion of AD 43 was trade and *oppida* were absolutely essential in this being the focus for multi-membership of communities both local and distant. The everyday life of these settlements depended on trade and the only way that the elites of the *oppida* could maintain it was by being one of those communities that became a member of the multi-membership of the Roman Empire. As such, it was inevitable that the elites would aspire to become Roman as this would maintain their position in their local communities and also persuade the occupiers to allow traditional practices to continue. Becoming Roman was beginning to happen willingly from the inside. The occupiers were quite content with the scenario and allowed it to continue for at least a decade before either their influence became more persuasive or the motivations of later Iron Age elites became stronger. The deciding factor may well have been the death of a leader whose trappings of later Iron Age power were buried with him such as that at Folly Lane or Tar barrows. The fact that there was no attempt to change the siting of places of power indicates that it was important not to reposition influential individuals and communities in relation to already existing patterns of movement, mobility and circulation and that these individuals were happy to support this strategy. Bagendon was different in that its situation was due to physcial reasons and again it may be that the Cirencester area was important in essential ways during the later Iron Age since it continued to develop into Corinium. However, there was also the fortress at Kingsholm to contend with and it is difficult to know what effect this may have had.

In terms of the later Iron Age landscape and politics, the military option seems a clumsy and unsophisticated scenario. Rather than accept the accounts of the military-driven occupation of southern Britain, which are based on problematic literary sources and result in a proto-historically driven archaeology, the study of

Akeman Street above suggests that the Roman approach in the early years after AD 43 is one of forming pragmatic, opportunist and flexible relationships with each area of the country, and these policies were likely to have been in place for some time before that event. While literary accounts extol the Roman conquest, and indicate a sharp break at AD 43, the archaeology points to a more subtle relationship between the Roman authorities and later Iron Age communities. The lack of forts along Akeman Street and the continued development of pre-Invasion social groups indicates that important personages and communities had already made pacts with Rome and had for some time been in some sort of political and economic relationship with the Empire, that they had special status, and therefore would not have put up any resistance to the conquering army.

The overall picture that emerges is one of continuity between the later Iron Age and the early Roman period in terms of routes and settlement along the Akeman Street corridor. If the concept of the *oppida* being economic 'multi-members' of the communities that they traded with is correct, the building of the Akeman Street spur from Alchester to the west would have changed discrete trading identities in valleys separated by their watersheds into the later Iron Age *oppida* formng constellations and multi-members of the growing province, with these changes being driven internally by elites. It was not the trade routes in the landscape that were to change, for the valley routes appear to have remained in use throughout the Roman period. The new man-made contribution to this geography was the appropriation of wealth from those discrete valley routes through the construction of routes over watersheds between *oppida*. This was a measure of continuity with later Iron Age centres of elite power becoming *civitas* capitals, rich rural sites becoming palatial villas. The only new aspect to this settlement geography were the roadside settlements built to service travellers, and the site of Alchester, intrusive into the later Iron Age pattern with its military foundation.

The date of Akeman Street has usually been placed in the late AD 40s, and perhaps that can be suggested for the Verulamium to Alchester and then north route. However, it would not be surprising to produce a later date for the section between Alchester and Corinium, perhaps the early AD 50s, and in terms of its fundamental importance in joining the Grim's Ditch area directly with Corinium a later date might be the most attractive proposition. The distribution of Roman roads in southern England, as envisaged by Margary, need not all have been constructed in the same period.

6

THE LATER FIRST AND EARLY SECOND CENTURIES

Laurence suggests the Roman road throughout Italy was a mechanism that reshaped the landscape after Roman control had initially been asserted through military intervention (1999, 197). This concept of the altered nature of space was the result of mobility and movement within the landscape through connecting places with different geographies. The views expressed here consider that military intervention was implicit rather than explicit along Akeman Street. How and why did increased movement and mobility influence individual landscapes, structures, trade and the resulting identity modification, if at all?

VERULAMIUM

It is difficult to assess the size of the early post-Boudiccan occupation area of Verulamium due to the insubstantiality of the structures or the fact that they rested on sill beams and while the inhabitants were constructing a new centre, they are likely to have been living in fairly ramshackle, temporary structures using what materials had survived the uprising. After the Boudiccan Revolt and the partial destruction of the town, the later first century was certainly a time of major building projects such as the forum/basilica complex completed in AD 79 dated by an inscription and overlying the aristocratic occupation site of c.AD 43. The *macellum* appears to have been built in the mid AD 80s and the baths dates are not exact but of this phase, and were certainly in existence by the late Flavian period. Some large temples were constructed about AD 100, although they were probably on sites previously used for religious purposes. Water supply, street grid, and drainage also had been provided by AD 100.

Excavation has demonstrated that by the late first and early second centuries, the area within the '1955' ditch was being steadily built up with a wide variety of private houses, constructed in different styles using timber, flint and mortar footings or a combination of both. However the town, approaching 75ha in AD 75-80, was never densely built up and most late first-century domestic structures appear to have been used for small-scale industry, especially metalworking, and interspersed with open land, sometimes being erected on the sites of pre-Boudiccan structures. The land that interspersed the settlement may have been used for paddocks, gardens common ground with the owners of adjacent houses, possibly with family connections.

The Fosse, here considered to have been part of the later Iron Age *oppida*, came into the limits of the town in the period AD 125-50, which enclosed an area of over 200ha. So, while the settlement in the valley was still a 'communal' area, it had changed character with the Catuvellaunian elite proclaiming the importance of their 'tribal capital' not through the monumentality of dykes and ditches but through that of Roman-style structures. However, the Fosse provided continuity that may well have been symbolic in some way.

It was Watling Street with its north–south axis that became the important route in this period, connecting with Londinium, the newly designated capital of the province and just one day away by horse, and then moving on to the Channel coast. The importance of the pre-Roman Akeman Street as the main thoroughfare through the valley was replaced although it is highly likely that it maintained it course through the valley from the east of Gorhambury. The changes in priorities can be seen in the construction of the London and Chester gates which have been dated to AD 117-38 and AD 140-60. They were expressly designed to impress with their enormous projecting gatehouses, constructed of flint and mortar and probably faced with sandstone, towering over the road and almost certainly bearing an inscription above the gateways.

Still hanging over valley of the Ver was Gorhambury. The early Roman rectangular structure seems to have been of one conception with those being built in the Verulamium below in the valley. It was a distinct sign of Roman influence in architecture, if not in the adoption of social lifestyles. After the Boudiccan rebellion a circular hut was contemporary with the reoccupation though it may have been part of a bigger complex due to traces of the rectangular structure being found close by. By the late first or early second century, Gorhambury had a fine structure of five rooms with a wing room on the north-east. Indications of great luxury are evidenced by a polygonal apse in the cellar, and stucco mouldings of half-scale figures, possibly a woman and child, painted with lifelike detail and colour. A mosaic also seems to have been in one of the rooms, and the standard of life was higher than anything being constructed in the town at this period. Curiously, in the later second century, the villa changed orientation from the east to the west when it was extended by five rooms. The structure was still in a position to dominate the skyline east of Verulamium, but, along with the shrine described below, it appears that its owners wanted to use its imposing façade to be on Akeman Street and instead of only dominating the skyline from the valley bottom thereby emphasising the route to the west.

THE GADE AND BULBOURNE VALLEYS

There is little doubt that the road from Cow Roast was still in use and that trading from the north to west still took place, but it appears to have declined in importance by the mid second century. That the route was still maintained and significant can be suggested by the shrine at Wood Lane End, Hemel Hempstead (Neal 1984, 193-215). First-century activity, not necessarily represented by buildings, may have indicated a native sacred spot such as a grove and certainly by the middle of the second century a sanctuary, possibly with a mausoleum, was arranged in a ditched enclosure and it is suspected that this might have been related to the family living at Gorhambury. The existence of this important structure, demonstrating the continuing power of a leading family, indicates that the Akeman Street later Iron Age route was still important (*23*).

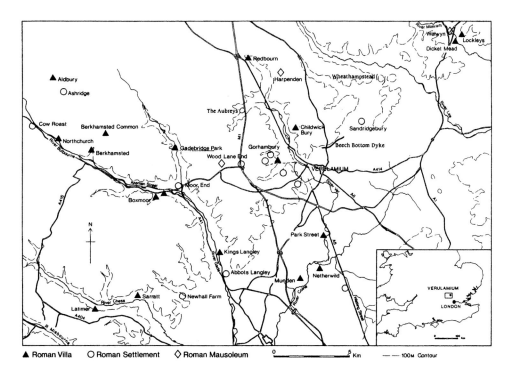

23 Villas and river systems around Verulamium (after Neal *et al.*)

The distribution of villa sites at regular intervals in the Bulbourne, Gade, Ver, Coln and Chess valleys west of Verulamium suggests some sort of planning control, but a similar effect might have been produced by the availability of water and the richness of the land. Nineteen villa-type buildings have been recognised over an area of 20 sq km west of the town along with two major settlements, one in the Glade valley and the other at Northchurch in the Bulbourne valley. Each of the rivers that formed the valleys are fairly fast-flowing rivers fed by numerous streams, but the extent of their navigability as a means for transporting produce is uncertain. Probably the River Gade as far as its confluence with the River Ver might have been used as a waterway. The Bulbourne valley as both a later Iron Age and early Roman communication route is rather different from the course of Akeman Street further west in that it has remained an important road through the Chilterns with both the Grand Union Canal and the mainline railway from London to Northampton following the line. There were three major villas in the Bulbourne valley, Boxmoor and Northchurch, and Gadebridge just 3.5km north of Boxmoor in the Gade valley. None of the sites had any trace of pre-conquest development.

GADEBRIDGE

Little is known about the early development of Gadebridge except that its main centre of occupation was probably to the east of the later site, and was a timber structure and an associated bathhouse of three rooms. In the second century the owners of Gadebridge villa embarked on an ambitious programme with the structure laid out as a 42m range of rooms with projecting wings and surrounded on all sides by a corridor. The plan of the house, like Boxmoor, was symmetrical and in the south-east wing was a cellar where there were three piers which probably once supported arcading designed to support a wall in the upper storey. By the end of the second century, Gadebridge was provided with two outer wings, the eastern of which joined the main house.

BOXMOOR

A timber house existed on the site towards the end of the first century; although small, it had five rooms with the wing rooms all surrounded by a corridor, an unusually early use of such architectural details. Although the walls were constructed of daub set on sleeper beams, one had painted plaster, a feature with some continuity in the villa's history. After the timber building was destroyed by fire a new one was constructed of stone and had 10 rooms, including wing rooms on the south side and provided with a hypocaust. In the middle of the second century two further rooms were added, on the east and north-east, and two mosaics were laid. It was a luxurious establishment with painted plaster depicting cupid-like figures and columns trailed with tendrils.

NORTHCHURCH

Excavated in 1973, the villa lies on the north bank of the Bulbourne, 1.5km south-east of Cow Roast. Although close to the water and liable to flooding and subsidence, the site was first occupied in the period AD 60-75. A simple masonry house of four rooms and corridor was put up in the early second century and rebuilt with 10 rooms a few decades later, only to be abandoned c.AD 170. It may have had a bath building.

COW ROAST/ASHRIDGE

Substantial evidence in terms of pits, wells and ditches and a range of artefact types suggests the continuing occupation from the first century to the fourth, though coin distribution indicates that the site was at the height of its prosperity in the middle of the second century. It is likely that the activities indicate a substantial roadside settlement with occupation spread over c.40ha with the main street aligned at 90 degrees to Akeman Street, though shops and facilities for travellers were likely to be situated along the Akeman Street frontage. Although marketing of agricultural products, particularly livestock, seems to have been important, it is the intense evidence for iron production that is paramount.

Above Cow Roast on the Ashridge plateau there is also a considerable amount of evidence for the mining of bog-ore in terms of shafts within the peasant agricultural landscape. The evidence of ironworking is in frequent finds of slag in surface scatters, particularly in the areas nearest the Bulbourne valley. Clearly the woods on the plateau above were still being managed effectively and efficiently through new planting and coppicing and so continuing the supply area of large amounts of charcoal that iron smelting requires. The bog-ore was transported down the steep slopes from the valley below and added to that mined in the valley bottom. Presumably, as in the earlier periods, processing the ore took place in the valley below and is evidenced by well shafts, pits, beam slots and bowl furnaces with tap-slag, hearths and smithing waste. Perhaps the most significant aspect of Cow Roast besides the manufacturing industry is the putative presence of a temple known from aerial photography. This site may have stood in a precinct with the settlement to either side, providing a ritual focus at the head of a river, and may have had pre-Roman origins. It would be a mistake to suggest that Cow Roast was primarily an industrial site as such, this type of activity may well have been bound up with other social aspects, including ritual factors (Zeepvat 1997). All of the villa structures along the Bulbourne valley may have been intimately related to both the

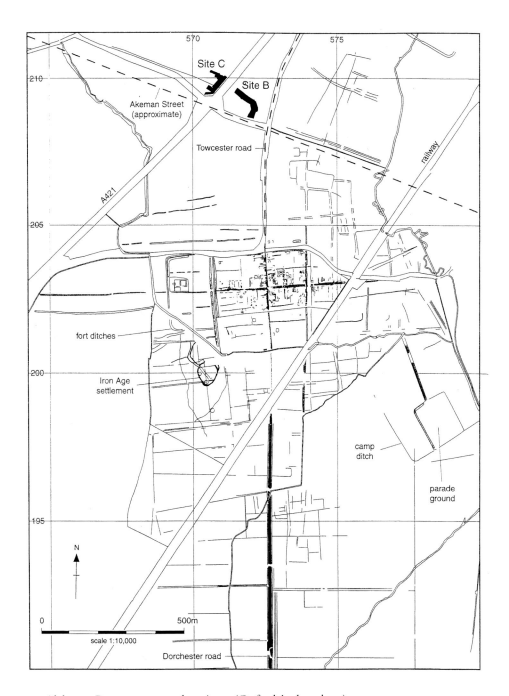

24 Alchester Roman town and environs (Oxford Archaeology)

kilns and types of vessel when plotted onto a map of the Midlands and Cotswold area matches very closely the routes emanating from Alchester. Even though a very rural landscape is suggested north of Alchester town, the sophistication of the roadside sprawl is indicated by the incidence of coinage, amphorae, glass and oysters and indicate the importance of the roads converging on the position, as fieldwalking on roadside settlements between Alchester and Bierton does not produce the same range of finds.

ALCHESTER

The main settlement at Alchester, east of the previous military establishment, is halfway along the route of Akeman Street and at the junction of several major routes, one to Dorchester another to Towcester and possibly a third to Alcester and on to Droitwich. The actual site of the town has been unoccupied since Roman times, resulting in heavy ploughing, seen in the lack of raised features except the ridge and furrow which has combed the southern portion. The site's relationship to Akeman Street is complex, there does seem to be an east–west branch forming one of the two main streets in the town, but the main axis of the settlement is the north–south road from Dorchester. There has been limited archaeological fieldwork undertaken within the walls at Alchester, with excavations in 1776, the mid 1880s, the 1920s and 1974 being small-scale and located in the north-east section of the site. These interventions have indicated that the late second century town ramparts enclose an almost square area of 10.5ha which together with its low-lying position on gravel sub-soil overlying Oxford clay would have made it prone to winter flooding. The defences comprised a stone wall, a bank-fronted berm and a shallow U-shaped ditch which were constructed as one in the late second century. The U shape of the ditch was unusual, but in such sodden ground it was probably impossible to dig the usual V-shaped defensive ditch, and this feature would probably have the nature of a continually flooded 'moat'. In 1928 substantial internal angle towers and substantial masonry gates were similarly demonstrated to be part of the same build as the bank behind. It is likely that the walled circuit did not have a defensive function, rather it indicated the demarcation between 'official' and private/public areas. A similar construction sequence has been found at Towcester which is Alchester's immediate neighbour to the north, and possibly at Alcester also with postulated late second-century defences, but in each case the dating evidence is quite sparse. Since similar walls of similar dates can be seen at the three locations it might be speculated that they are related to uprisings among the local populations and that the walls were built to secure areas of a settlement whose function had been important to the province. What is significant here is that there have been indications across the site of previous, pre-wall structures and several 'levellings-up' to produce ground surfaces which would be above the water table all year. The earlier settlement, which does not appear to have been related to the early military establishment(s), was much more extensive and it would appear that it was only the central part that was later walled. Such an area was more substantial than those typical of a small town whose type has been regarded as just a market centre.

Excavation and aerial photography have demonstrated a regularly planned site, unlike most small towns, and, although an inter-vallum road has been detected, large areas of the town do not seem to have been built on. Excavations have mainly been undertaken around the central crossroads and revealed a number of structures indicating a set of buildings of some importance, but there is no obvious explanation for their purpose or occupation. Evidence for a building on the north-east angle points to an important structure with the courtyard open to the south, surrounded on three sides by a corridor, the outer walls of which supported by shallow pilaster buttresses. The corridor was paved with *opus signinum* and traces of wall plaster and roof tiling were unearthed. Finds from fieldwalking have produced evidence of a high-status settlement – statuettes, painted wall plaster, ornate and expensive personal items and fine pottery. However, there were some unique and informative features which have been captured in a series of aerial photographs taken on eight occasions between 1926 and 1979. The images indicated a large rectangular structure to the west of the crossroads, the function of which is obscure. It might have been a market area, a small and crowded one, but it also looks very similar in shape to the 'state' temple at Verulamium at the rear of the front of the forum/basilica. There were also at least two other possible temples in the town, a Romano-Celtic rectangular structure and a circular building. A possible *mansio* stood near the west gate. To the west of, and outside, the ramparts is a mound known as 'Castle Hill' under which the remains of a mosaic pavement and hypocaust were unearthed in 1766, and which appears to be the site of a bath house.

That such a demographically small settlement had such imposing walls suggests that it had an administrative or military function. Presumably the Roman Army in Britannia had to have such central depots to collect materials for forts on the northern frontiers and/or there needed to be some supervision of the road system to ensure that its upkeep was regular and consistent (the significance of the location of Alchester is echoed today by the Central Ordnance Depot of the British Army established in 1941 nearby to the east along the line of Akeman Street). It has been proposed on several occasions that Alchester was the base, or one of the bases, of a *beneficiarius consularis* who undertook the role of monitoring the quality of the roads. If this hypothesis is accepted then one would expect that there would be official buildings and storehouses within the settlement and it might not have been completely built over due to space needed for hard standing. Finds of military materials from excavations near the major Akeman Street/Dorchester to Towcester crossroads might indicate also a second-century military post connected with the role of the officials based in the town or using it as a base for perambulations. That part of an illegible inscription was also discovered near to the site might support this interpretation. The presence of markets outside the town, particularly on the Akeman Street 'bypass', may well have been because of the restricted nature of the land at the heart of the settlement later enclosed by walls.

Such a significant number of temples within such a small area is surprising and adds to the possibility that Alchester was a special sort of regional centre with a role that was wider than a market town, perhaps playing part of the role of a regional *civitas* capital halfway between the two major administrative market centres of Verulamium and Corinium. If the Grim's Ditch area was seen as an estate belonging to a group who were not included in either the *civitas* of the Dobunni or Catuvellauni, then the need for an administrative centre outside it would have been vital.

SANSOM'S PLATT

The settlement at Sansom's Platt lies 750m west of the Glyme and therefore about 1.5km from Phase Two of the Grim's Ditch earthwork, and is very different from the other small settlements in the Grim's Ditch area (*25*). It was discovered in a pipeline trench in 1972 after Roman material including pottery and coins found since 1894 indicated that a watching brief should be mounted. The site was originally identified as a villa after the discovery of at least three rooms, including one with painted wall plaster and a red concrete floor. Finds from the site indicated a date range from the first to the third century AD. The discovery of another structure a short distance to the north-west indicated a larger site than was previously thought. Aerial photographs that were taken in the highly favourable conditions of 1996 identified the layout of a small settlement and subsequent fieldwalking has produced significant quantities of Iron Age as well as early Roman pottery, indicating a site of some importance to promote such continuity. The settlement was set back off the Roman road, its axis being a south-western street. One of the earliest Roman features appears to be a large sub-rectangular enclosure with a developed winged corridor type of plan with the later central road and some shops impinging on its southern boundary wall. However, without excavation this relative chronology cannot be more closely ascertained. If it is a villa it is in a totally different position from other villas in the area which are away from the road as is typical in southern England. It has been suggested that the site is that of a *mansio*, where official travellers (passports were required for identification) found a complete villa dedicated to their refreshment and a staging place for a change of horses. Alternatively, the Samson's Platt site may have possibly been *mutation* ('changing station'), a posting station for the *mutationes* and located every 12-18 miles. In these complexes the driver could purchase the services of wheelrights, cartwrights, and *equarii medici*, or veterinarians. A problem with the identification of Sansom's Platt as a *mansio* is its closeness to Alchester. A

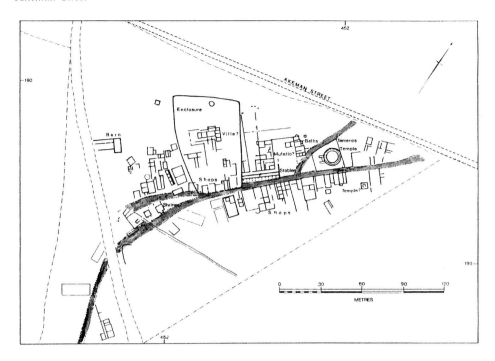

25 Sansom's Platt, Tackley – plan reconstructed from aerial photographs (Richard Massey)

mansio might also have been located at this point because on entering the Grim's Ditch complex there would appear to be no other roadside settlements besides Wilcote, which served a very different function, and perhaps this indicates that the area was regarded as a private estate which although tolerating a narrowed road through it discouraged opportunities for stopping.

The most marked feature of the settlement at Sansom's Platt is a large circular temple, 20m in diameter with a *tremolos* in the fork of the road, which was at the head of the main street and also easily visible from Akeman Street. At least two square shrines, which look distinctively later Iron Age, also appear to be in the fork of the road at the south-west corner of the settlement and bear some resemblances with structures at temples such as Lydney and Uley. However, the major temple structure seems to have been of some pretensions and probably showed a wealth of architectural detail, possibly of early second- or third-century origin. The presence of a bath house encroaching slightly onto the axial road might suggest that this was a place of pilgrimage.

While there may be shops in the strip buildings fronting the road, there is at present no area identified that would be big enough to act as a market. However if travel within the Grim's Ditch area was discouraged then at some locality close to Sansom's Platt there may have been a site which acted as a north/south market for villas and other agricultural establishments to the north. This function might have been fulfilled by a substantial settlement on the western side of the Glyme at the entrance to the Phase Two of the Grim's Ditch from which a large scatter of first- to third-century pottery and materials was recovered during fieldwalking in advance of the proposed contruction of the Woodstock bypass.

THE NORTH OXFORDSHIRE GRIM'S DITCH

While the earthworks of this feature must have been still highly visible in the landscape there is no convincing evidence for a re-cutting of the ditch or the replacement of a palisade. However, considering the number of early villas within the boundaries of the degrading earthwork it would appear that it was still acting as a significant social, and perhaps political, boundary (*26*). The relationships between these high-status sites and those of the later Iron Age demonstrate a continuity of status and economic power. There is one site among these early Roman structures, Stonesfield Roman 'villa', that is enigmatic and unfortunately cannot be dated as it was totally destroyed in the eighteenth and nineteenth centuries. Its exact location is now lost but its position was alongside Akeman Street just a few hundred metres from the road and in full view of it. What is also significant is that it had a view over the Evenlode valley taking in most of the area of Phase Two of the Grim's Ditch. This was complementary to a site with a similar panoramic view at Wilcote on the other side of the valley. There is evidence of the Stonesfield structure's importance in the fourth century with the discovery and recording of a huge Bacchus mosaic pavement which may indicate a ritual function. Evidence for the presence of a shrine is suggested also at the Wilcote site.

CALLOW HILL

The villa straddles the B4437 on the road from Charlbury to Woodstock and is set in an enclosure about 128m from north to south and *c.*192m from west to east. It lies close to elements of Grim's Ditch, as seen above, and was on the site of a significant Iron Age settlement of some pretensions. Lane-Fox recognised it in 1868 as the site of a villa, describing it as 'the remains of a rectangular enclosure thickly strewed with Roman tiles and pottery.' In 1916 a floor 'partly painted in red, green and black' about 3.5-4.5 sq m was broken with a pick, when foundations and coloured plaster were also found. The villa enclosure, with internal well, was identified by Allen from the air in 1933-6 in a series of oblique photographs. In 1939 in the *Victoria County History* it was reported that the house site could be distinctly seen when the crop was off, and that potsherds and *tesserae* from a mosaic could be collected. Thomas, in 1950, trenched the villa enclosure, finding a surrounding ditch which was flat-bottomed and

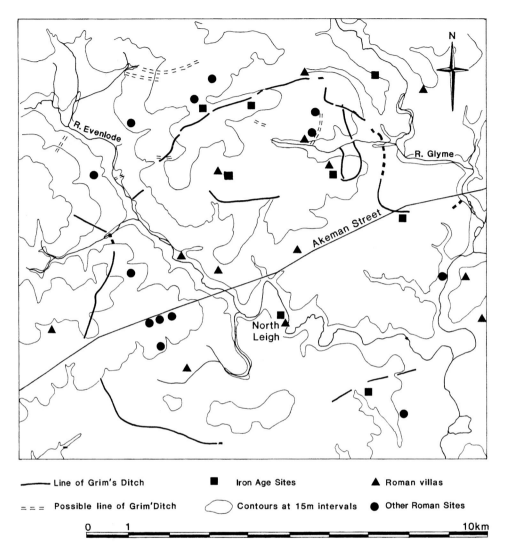

26 Iron-Age and Roman settlement in the Grim's Ditch area

vertical-sided, which he interpreted as being for defence, and also found post holes for a gate. Thomas suggested that the ditch had been cut in the second half of the first century AD and that the villa may have been rebuilt in stone in the early second century. He surmised from the pottery retrieved that the site had been occupied until the end of the Roman period. Today, ploughing has destroyed any evidence for the villa, and made any further work unprofitable. However, Massey has interpreted a feature in aerial photographs as a mausoleum of some kind within the walled area.

DITCHLEY

Radford (1936) identified evidence for four phases in the main structure at Ditchley villa. The first house had been erected about AD 80 and was a rough timber structure 14.6m by 9.8m, and was recognised by 17 post holes, the contents of which had been removed in the further development of the house. As suggested previously, the shape of the early house can be interpreted as a stylised banjo enclosure enshrining in memory the site that existed on the slope above it. It was likely that the walls of the structure were of wattle and daub and the excavator suggested that they carried a hipped roof of thatch and accommodated both cattle as well as humans. The early house was set in the upper part of a courtyard over 91.4 sq m, enclosed by a V-shaped ditch, and it is probable that a bank was formed from the upcast. An entrance in the south side was 15.2m wide and just within it on the west was a possible small timber-framed building.

In the early second century Radford proposed that the wooden structure was succeeded by a substantial one-storied stone house, some 28.7m by 14.9m, with walls of locally quarried stone, resting on heavy foundations built to the south to level the area. It was roofed with tiles and contained six rooms, with two wings projecting southwards at each end, connected by a veranda carried on wooden posts. Radford suggested that the entrance was by three steps into the eastern wing, the first room of which may have been an open portico. The portico led to the most important room which had a kitchen behind with an open central hearth. West of the kitchen may have been serving rooms and beyond them a room, the width of the building, opened onto the veranda. Two rooms which formed the westerly wing were probably private rooms. The walls were plastered and painted and the windows glazed. The floors probably rested on wooden joists. Shortly after its construction a row of rooms was added to the north including a new kitchen, possible baths where water might have been thrown onto hot stones thereby producing steam, and other rooms perhaps for servants all connected by a central corridor. A well, probably timber-lined and covered with a well house, was built in the centre of the courtyard and remained in use until it silted up at the end of the fourth century. West of the well was a circular structure 9.4m across, with pitched foundations surrounding a cobbled area, which was interpreted as a kerbed threshing floor; however, circular features within early villas are increasingly interpreted as being some sort of commemoration of later Iron Age houses. Across the south end of the courtyard there had been extensive outbuildings that suffered much destruction, particularly to the west. The excavator identified a structure measuring 85.3m by 21.3m covering the west side. It was timber-framed, with wattle and daub walls and roofed with thatch, and was interpreted as the labourers' quarters. There were two enclosures outside the main ditch and these were interpreted as probably containing orchards or gardens.

FAWLER

Excavations by Oxford Archaeological Unit at the villa in 1986 established that extensive early Roman occupation, indicated by pottery of the mid or late first century, was evidence of the first colonisation of the site. A dog burial accompanied by a wine flagon suggested a ritual act in this early period. A first phase building was dated to the first or early second century AD, and was represented by a wall and debris which included painted wall plaster and blue-glass *tesserae*. Other finds from this phase, including a silvered brooch, suggested that the occupation was of high status from the outset rather than growing from modest origins. A building beside the Evenlode, probably a bath house was dated to the second century. The debris from the structure indicated that it had a hypocaust, with tessellated floors, painted walls and a tufa ceiling.

WILCOTE

Wilcote is a very enigmatic settlement. After the initial building of Akeman Street, stone appears to have been continued to be quarried for the road well into the second century. The nature of the friable rock outcrop was not good enough for building and roofing, and other quarries which provided building stone, i.e. those in the Windrush valley, would have had only waste material for use on roads. The quarries at Wilcote therefore might have provided stone for quite a large stretch of Akeman Street. Clay was also quarried, perhaps for brick or tile manufacture.

The settlement, a strip of *c.*600m in places, along the south side the road and *c.*50m deep, appears to have experienced continuous growth through the later first century up to the middle of the second century which could be related to the growth of towns and settlements along Akeman Street. This might have led to increased traffic, both local and regional, with increased opportunities for trade and the supply of goods and services to travellers, while the establishment and growth of local villas would have meant that Wilcote could have become a trading mediator for the increasing wealthy hinterland.

It is a very different settlement from those either side of it on Akeman Street. As has already been discussed, Sansom's Platt is much more complex containing both main streets and side streets and possibly having an important religious role. There is a similar complexity about Asthall. However, Wilcote does not seem to have had an independence directly related to the road, except perhaps in its maintenance. It is sited in a poor position with poor access to water and its structures generally appear to be largely post-built lengthways to the road.

The relationship of Wilcote with the surrounding villas is difficult to determine. Certainly Shakenoak was a 'working' villa (a 'home farm?'), though it is not possible to conclude this about North Leigh, the entrance drive of which appears to leave Akeman Street at Wilcote. North Leigh villa may well have acquired its wealth from the local villas but it is more likely that much of it came from extensive properties in the Thames valley where dense areas of farming settlements and villages lie just 10km to the south. The wider landscape still seems to have continued the pattern of the later Iron Age settlement with three distinct distributions in the upper Thames region which suggest three distinct clusters. Two elongated clusters defined the dense concentrations of settlement on the upper Thames gravels, extending from Oxford to the area forming the inter-fluvial land around Lechlade and with the other major concentration of settlement being the area immediately west of the Cherwell and occupying the area of the North Oxfordshire Grim's Ditch between the river valleys of the Glyme and Evenlode.

While Wilcote could have acted as a reservoir for seasonal labour, it is best seen as still being related to ensuring that Akeman Street was well surfaced thereby demonstrating the wealth of the villa settlements who would have been responsible for maintenance. There is evidence of slaughter of both cattle and sheep at Wilcote in the number of bones and a cattle goad for herding of cattle through the site. However, within the narrow strip of land either side of the main road it would appear that only subsistence agriculture was possible. A possible tile kiln may have existed at the western end of the site although the longevity of this feature may have been short once the early villas were completed and then as they prospered turned to the higher status, and seeming exclusivity, of Stonesfield slate. Evidence of metalworking is seen in a pair of long-jawed iron tongs and the identification of small hearths, but it would appear from the lack of slag that most ironworking took place some distance from the northern part of Wilcote.

Considering the present knowledge of the extent and quality of the structures, it is unlikely that the settlement had a role as a market or roadside settlement in any developed form. Certainly there was some manufacture and repair of goods, for different consumers – the inhabitants, travellers, and trade at a distance. As has been emphasised for the later Iron Age landscape, the main relationships may not have been east–west but north–south, the present pattern of the roads and lanes in the area, especially around Wilcote, reflecting this and therefore the axis of the major trade was towards the Thames. Both Sansom's Platt and Asthall have these north–south connections, and their importance might be better seen in this light rather than in relation to Akeman Street.

There remains the problem of the number of high-status goods found alongside the road at Wilcote: Gaulish and Rhineland imports, mortaria from northern Gaul as well as Mancetter-Hartshill to the north and Verulamium to the east. As the excavator has pointed out, there seems to be no use of these products at nearby Shakenoak, and a significant amount of the imported fine wares predate the villas. Amphorae, especially early-Roman dated styles, have also been found and have raised suggestions of a Roman fort in the area. An unexpected find at the Wilcote site was the incidence of votive artefacts – damaged model and reworked objects – with evidence of scrap metal and metalworking. These types of artefacts can be paralleled with others from temple sites. The location of any such temple has yet to be discovered, however, finds of box-flue tiles, Purbeck marble wall veneer and painted wall plaster indicate a very high-status structure that was certainly in use in the early second century and may have been the reason for the high-status material alongside the road. An important factor in any ritual structure's siting may have been that from the upper end of the Wilcote locality the whole of the area of Phase Two of the Grim's Ditch can be seen, as can the site of the Stonesfield villa in a similar position on the opposite side of the territory. The uninterrupted view from this point was also responsible for the siting of an eponymous Second World War airfield on Akeman Street, with the course of the road running through its middle.

NORTH LEIGH

Lack of dating evidence due to poorly recorded antiquarian and later excavation means that this villa is best dealt with in relative structural periods (Wilson and Sherlock 1980). The earliest buildings in Roman style on or close to a significant later Iron Age site were probably single-storied, as they were throughout the villa's history, and were constructed either in the late first century or in the early second century under the walls and floors of the later north-west range. The main house was 20.3m long, originally containing a row of five rooms with a south-facing front composed of a colonnaded passage between two projecting wings. At a later date the front was modified with the extension of the passage and the insertion of a mosaic pavement of a simple geometric design in red and white. South-west of the main structure was a barn possibly of aisled construction. Later a corridor or covered passage was added to the south-eastern side and red and white mosaic, similar to that in the main house, was inserted. These alterations suggest that the structure was used for domestic as well as agricultural purposes, and the similarity of alterations in both buildings indicate an attempt to make them architecturally harmonious. This was continued in the connection of both buildings by adding two new rooms between them and allowing direct access from one to the other. North-east of the main structure was a bath building, the North Baths, which provided with an undressing room, cool and warm rooms and a cold plunge bath. This structure has not been completely excavated. Roofing in all phases of the villa appears to be of stone from nearby Stonesfield. The use of Stonesfield slate is restricted to the Grim's Ditch area and although excellent the roofing material does not seem to travel far, despite the fact that Akeman Street runs within several hundred metres of the mines. It may be that its use was deliberately restricted for some reason, perhaps related to the presence of the prestigious villas at North Leigh and Fawler being close, or as a sign of distinction for the group within the Grim's Ditch earthworks.

SHAKENOAK

The first published reference to the site was in the *Victoria County History* (1939) which described the presence of tiles with mortar adhering stamped with a rectangular pattern, coloured plaster and one pillar of a hypocaust on each side of a brook at Shakenoak Farm, near North Leigh village. Excavation of the site was undertaken annually from 1960–7 and remains the most complete recent villa excavation along the whole of Akeman Street, though some of the excavator's conclusions have been challenged by other archaeologists (Brodribb, Hands and Walker 1992-7). The excavators considered that occupation at Shakenoak was probably continuous from the last quarter of the first century AD to the middle of the eighth century. Evidence of activity before AD 70 was from a small number of objects found in later deposits and the undated remains of a circular hut. The second century was a time of significant capital expenditure at Shakenoak and construction projects were conceived on a grand scale. A corridor house, dated between AD 70 and 90, lies to the north of the stream.

ASTHALL

The settlement sat astride Akeman Street, at the crossing of the Windrush, inside the sheltered location of an abandoned meander. With the building of Akeman Street, it is quite likely that the Roman authorities would encourage major settlements along the road, whilst other, more slight examples such as Wilcote would have grown up in response to market conditions (*27*). It is interesting that both the site on the putative Woodstock bypass and Asthall are both outside the Grim's Ditch earthworks which might indicate an exclusion from the interior. This would suggest that Wilcote had a different function.

Excavation in 1992 on the outskirts of the settlement showed the orientation of structures with their short axes to the street which indicates that street frontage was at a premium (Booth 1997). Parch marks indicate that the fronting was intensively built up on both sides, though the settlement was not symmetrical about its axis, but concentrated on its south-east side. Previous excavations had unearthed small cemeteries, two wells, roads and finds which included a votive miniature axe and bird of copper alloy indicating some sort of religious structure. A number of villas lie close to the Asthall settlement, though as yet there is no firm dating for them, and it is likely that they were attracted by the settlement. Their density is not as thick as other areas to the south and outside the Grim's Ditch circuit so it might be that they are also at the range of good-quality sheltered land. Their relationship to the Grim's Ditch pattern of settlement is unknown. Asthall small town clearly had the potential to be a market centre in a river valley, which was most probably part of an earlier north-west to south-east routeway, as has been seen throughout this study.

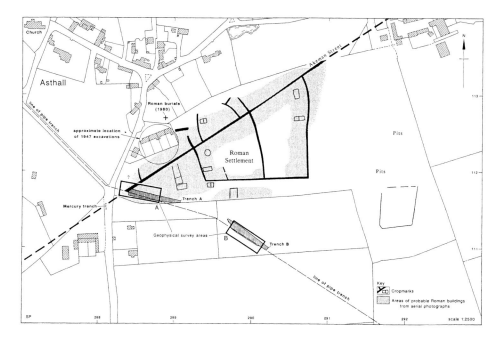

27 Asthall Roman settlement (Oxford Archaeology)

BARNSLEY VILLA (WELSH WAY STILL IN EXISTENCE)

The excavator of the Roman 'villa' admitted that the site and the surrounding earthworks were extremely difficult to interpret due to the many dry stone structures on an Oolitic limestone bedrock. The lack of stratification across the site made its dating extremely precarious and was based on a limited amount of information. While the first phase was dated to *c*.AD 140-275 what is interesting is the presence of four-post structures and the number of segments of circular features that look surprisingly like eaves-drip gullies of Iron Age round houses (Webster 1981) (*28*). Although only three fragments of Iron Age pottery were found some of the assemblage, particularly the Severn Valley Ware, have date ranges that have been considerably extended since 1961-79, and some of the Phase One pottery could well have been much earlier and of the later Iron Age period. Although Akeman Street was now in existence, probably as a metalled road, there is no reason why the Welsh Way route should not have existed as a bypass for Corinium for herding cattle from Ermine Street thereby keeping the Cirencester area traffic-free.

At this time the excavator suggested that there was a putative timber-framed house, a well and at least one curved ditch and nearby infant burials. It was in this

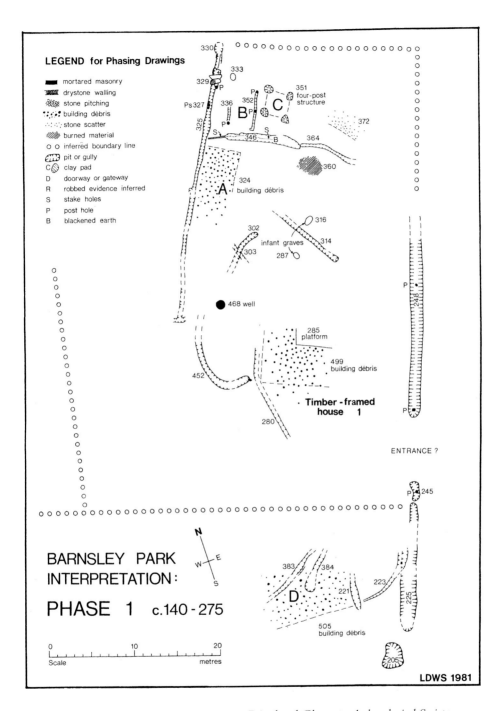

LEGEND for Phasing Drawings

- ▬ mortared masonry
- ▨ drystone walling
- ▧ stone pitching
- ∴ building débris
- ∴ stone scatter
- ▨ burned material
- ○ ○ inferred boundary line
- ⬭ pit or gully
- C ◎ clay pad
- D doorway or gateway
- R robbed evidence inferred
- S stake holes
- P post hole
- B blackened earth

330

333

329

Ps 327

336

352

351 four-post structure

B

C

325

346

B

372

364

360

A

324 building débris

302

316

303

287

infant graves

314

● 468 well

285 platform

499 building débris

452

Timber-framed house 1

280

ENTRANCE ?

P 245

BARNSLEY PARK INTERPRETATION:

N
W E
S

PHASE 1 c.140-275

383

384

223

D

221

225

505 building débris

0   10   20
Scale   metres

205

LDWS 1981

28 Barnsley Villa Phase One *c.* AD 140-275. *Bristol and Gloucester Archaeological Society Transaction Vol 99, p.30* 'phase' that the four-posted structure was uncovered, and although admitted as being typical of the late Iron Age suggested that at this period the occupants of the site were Britons who had absorbed some Romanising influence but also retained older traditions. This might well be the case, but one would expect some measure of continuity from the later Iron Age. Excavations indicated a large number of round dry-stone structures, thought to be pens of some sort, though they have been reinterpreted as a set of houses (Smith 1985). If these structures are of this date then there is a continuity of Iron Age settlement forms unexpectedly close to Akeman Street and Cirencester. However, even though they may be outlying structures of a developing villa building elsewhere, this is still a significant find.

BAGENDON

On present evidence it is likely that the settlement behind the Bagendon Dykes was abandoned in this period, although, again, we do not know what was happening below the present village. However, a spread of later occupation would be expected and it is most likely that this small settlement was out of use with its population moving elsewhere, probably to early Corinium, though it should not be considered that the move was enforced, but due to lack of trade passing along the Welsh Way.

DITCHES

The main villa block appears to have been built during the third quarter of the first century, at least by AD 80, and comprised of a 'row-type' house. By the mid to late first century there had been a timber veranda or corridor created which encompassed the whole building, which had by now been replaced in stone and to which wings had been added. As a more substantial building it was clearly visible from Ermine Street and no doubt the Welsh Way that must certainly have been in use as a bypass to Glevum. (In order not to pre-empt the publication of recent work so kindly sent to me, only the necessary details are given here.) However, it is highly likely that the Bagendon Dykes were now not used and therefore, perhaps with trade patterns changing, the Ditches had to make an even bigger statement of identity to the Roman Army by being visually prominent from Ermine Street. Continuity of ownership at Ditches indicates that the local elite wished to impress subordinates and forge financial and political links with a new administration.

That there was continuity in occupation of the site can hardly be doubted, and the significant question is occupation by whom? Had Gaulish traders moving upstream founded the *oppida*, or was it traders from the south coast who were also trading directly with Gaul and bringing modified identities with them?

AKEMAN STREET FROM BAGENDON TO CIRENCESTER

So far, the techniques of constructing Roman roads have not been discussed and have been taken for granted. However, the order of the construction of roads around Cirencester becomes an important issue in considering the archaeology of the area during its growth. Patterns of movement around the Roman town appear to be logically Roman and immediately post-conquest: Fosse Way from Isca at Exeter to Lindum at Lincoln, Ermine Street joining the early fort to Silchester and Gloucester.

However, Akeman Street appears to be incongruous joining a later route of Fosse Way to enter the town through the 'Verulamium' Gate. In an impressive study of the surveying of the roads entering Corinium, Hargreaves (1998) suggests that in the sequence of their construction the decision to build Akeman Street was just before the town's street grid was set up *c.*AD 70-85 (*29*). This could be seen as problematic since evidence for a broad mid first-century date has been suggested at Wilcote and Asthall. The position of Alchester as a military establishment and its relationship to the road is unclear and therefore to use the AD 44 dendro-date for the road would invite further problems. Holbrook has commented that perhaps Akeman Street was not surfaced until AD 70-85 and therefore any previous approach to the town site would not be visible in the landscape today. A 34-year wait between construction and surfacing invites comment about the importance of the route and its relationship with the short-lived forts at Corinium as they seemed to have been focused on Ermine Street with no obvious connection with Akeman Street. This discrepancy has been solved here by proposing that the Welsh Way was used as a major pre- and post-conquest route. The lateness of the imposition of the current suggested course of Akeman Street indicates there was no hurry to attract the local population to a Roman way of life. However, at the same time as proposed change takes place the Bagendon dykes settlement appears to have disappeared and Ditches changes its orientation, all possibly as a result of the Akeman Street change of course, though undoubtedly the Welsh Way remained as a bypass or cattle-droving route. The joining of the Fosse Way to Akeman Street can be explained by the eclipse in the importance of the former as towns on its route, such as Ratae at Leicester and Lindum at Lincoln, became successful in relationship to the north-west to south-east routes which made more economic sense than the course of a severely military route, and this was also reflected in the imposition of the Corinium street grid over the Fosse Way. The construction of Akeman Street altered the orientation of the settlement pattern also by bringing the influential elites of the North Oxfordshire Grim's Ditch into orbit of the precocious *civitas* capital. If anything personifies the development of the Province in this area it is this change of routes from Bagendon/Ditches/Duntisbournes to Corinium. If the name 'Corinium' has some connection with the 'Celtic' name for woods, it might be better to not think of the Bagendon settlement as being abandoned for Cirencester, but the Duntisbourne settlement,

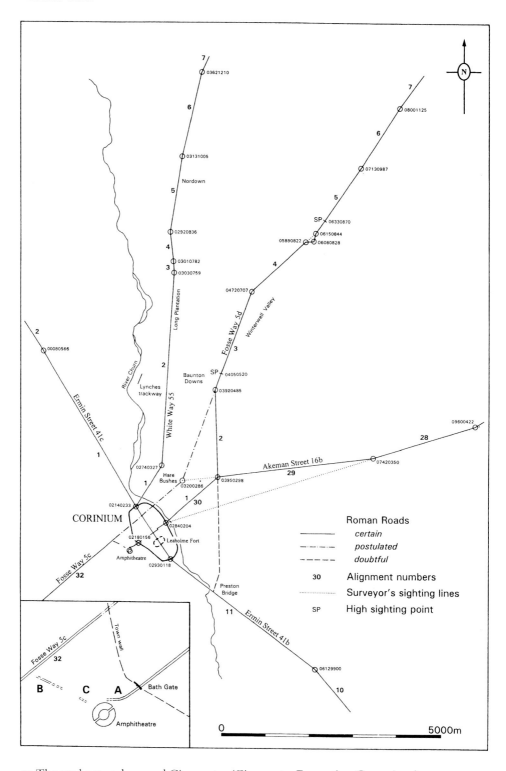

29 The road network around Cirencester (Cirencester Excavation Committee)

with its possible ritual connections suggested above, moving from the woods down Ermine Street.

CIRENCESTER: CORINIUM

Richard Reece, based on Hargreaves' observations, has noted (2003) that Corinium was in the 'wrong' location because of its propensity to flood. Reece considers that the 'better fit' area was not acceptable because of the presence of an important ritual site, perhaps connected to the Tar Barrows or their locality. However, the site eventually chosen for Corinium was intimately related to the stream beds of Daglingworth Brook and Churn and associated marshy areas, separated by a marshy island, and it may well be this association with water and marsh that was the reason for the choice of location. The circles of stakeholes underneath the fort site might be related to ritual processes, though the placing of a fort on top of them would seem to be a crass act. Considering the similar circumstances of the foundation of Verulamium, clearly choosing a site for a *civitas* capital involved a complex set of considerations regarding continuities of identity, ritual and power.

Like many other *civitas* capitals, Cirencester was slow in getting started and Reece has pointed out that Corinium took a long time to grow as there were already so many markets available to the early Roman population. The major public building programme and developed street grid may have occurred as a period which may have lasted for a much as three or four decades either side of AD 100 – the evidence is not as easily accessible as that at Verulamium. Corinium has been largely built over, its present plan based on the medieval town, and excavation is made more difficult by the number of later listed buildings exisiting above the Roman town (*30*). The street grid appears to have grown by accretion over a number of decades rather than *de novo*. This process may be responsible for the offset nature of some of the streets. It is also of interest that the road from the Verulamium Gate to the forum is offset so that the latter could not be seen from the front of the forum and this may well have something to do with pre-town settlement.

The public buildings included a basilica which had an aisled hall and a forum, the construction of both appears to have begun at about the same time as the street grid was set down. While a possible *mancellum* and theatre were built in the north-western part of the town there have been as yet no traces of bath buildings or temples located. Shops in the centre of the town originating as timber buildings were built in a piecemeal fashion in stone from the second century with the major roads having colonnaded rows along them. Those town houses that had been constructed appear to have been timber buildings until the middle of the second century, but domestic and civic structures took up less than half the space of the 96ha enclosed by an earthen bank of the late first/early second centuries.

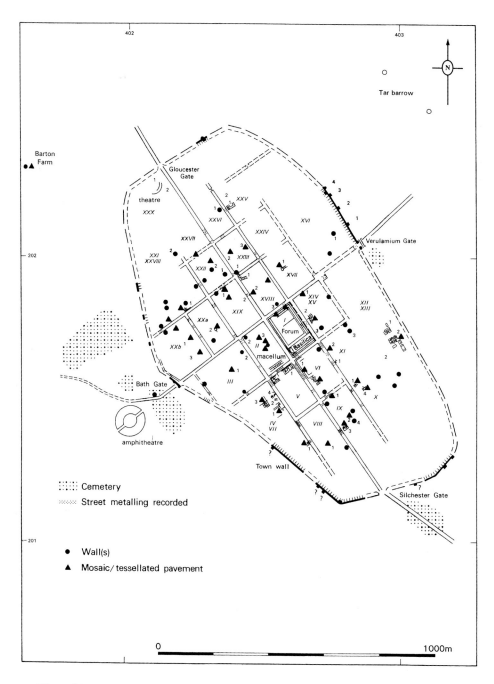

30 Plan of Cirencester (Cirencester Excavation Committee)

This definition of the town limits was an ambitious project making Corinium second only to London in area in the province of Britannia. By the middle of the second century stone gates were built into the banks, and significantly, one of the most important was that built over Akeman Street as it entered the town.

Reece and Catling (1975, 5) suggested that no alignment of Akeman Street approaching Corinium made very good sense as it came in from the east, and this together with the fact that this was the only Roman road to be severely dislocated in its path *out* of the town in later times, suggests this was a later, subsidiary Roman highway of limited use. Perhaps we should consider the experience of travellers coming *into* the town at the end of a journey in AD 160 in much the same way that journey was begun above Verlamion in Chapter 3. The importance of Akeman Street was determined in *c.*AD 70 when the Fosse Way and Akeman Street were brought together to approach the town in an almost choreographed processional way, an obviously prestigious military road with an obvious civilian one, with the latter now more important than the former.

Travellers approaching the Verulamium Gate of Corinium had already experienced the difference between the surface of the country tracks and that of the metalled Akeman Street, and administrative locations such as Alchester town, the *mansiones* and roadside towns all embodied the concern for permanency and efficiency, a constant reminder of the long arm of the State but also giving a sense of belonging between towns in the province. The straightness of the road would have impressed with its detailed surveying, defying the irregularities of the landscape. Another sense of the fundamental difference between Akeman Street and the tracks adjoining it were the milestones with their measurement of distance to towns not only giving a continuity between two places but also raising the anticipation of the traveller through the decreasing distance in miles to Corinium. Also inscribed on the milestones might have been the equivalent to the modern 'Roman Cirencester Capital of the Cotswolds' implying relationships with the capital of the Dobunni.

The importance of the town was hinted at by the forum and basilica hanging over the earthworks surrounding the town, but it was not until very close that the magnificence of the Verulamium Gate stunned the traveller. No doubt the oral tradition had already talked up the grandeur of the gateway, but this would have been totally unexpected. The dual carriageway within each of the double arches of the gate expressed the economic success of the town and the surrounding area. The ornate drum columns and string courses echoed another culture, that of Rome, and the statues in the niches high above congratulated the traveller on a successful journey and affirmed the gods' protection while in the town.

To the Governor processing through his province there would be reassuring echoes of Rome, even though the design of the forum and basilica was more suited to a warm climate than that of Britannia. To the merchant there was the mirror image of the entrance of Londinium Gate at Verulamium (*31*), which also produced comparison between the towns, and the repeated and predictable

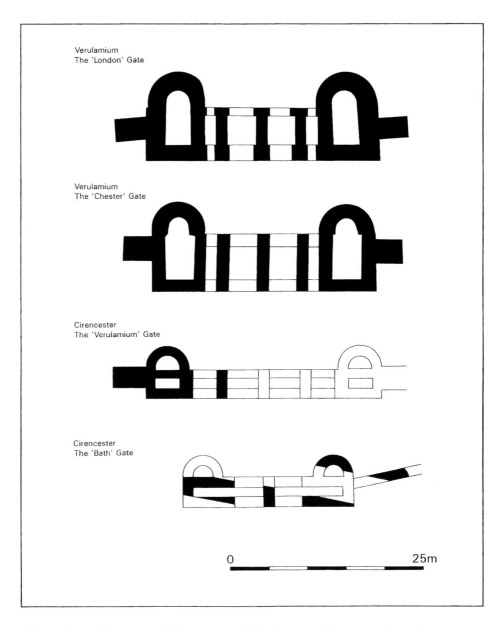

Verulamium
The 'London' Gate

Verulamium
The 'Chester' Gate

Cirencester
The 'Verulamium' Gate

Cirencester
The 'Bath' Gate

0   25m

31 Comparison of the gates of Cirencester and Verulamium (Cirencester Excavation Committee)

elements such as the forums and basilicas giving reassurance of prosperity and so relief that the journey and financial risks had been worth the effort. The wealthy from the Grim's Ditch area, just a few hours travel to their town residences, would have been satisfied that the city and the leading families had been encouraged in erecting the magnificent gate on 'their' side of the town and would have recognised that 'their' road was responsible for its wealth. To the peasant delivering goods to the markets inside Corinium, it was the echo underneath the gateway, not to be experienced anywhere else, that always thrilled and produced a sense of awe. Without Akeman Street these feelings could not be experienced and the road was as much a part of the townscape as the structures inside it. Without the road the structures would have been significant only to a small number of people, would lack sophisticated design and would never have developed to their extent.

7

BECOMING ROMAN ALONGSIDE AKEMAN STREET

Laurence (1990, 5) suggests that 'a new culture of both space and time' was responsible for a growth of space for imperialism and empire, where the road was as much a part of defining the Roman cultural landscape as it was of the city and the villa, and that the three were mutually dependent upon each other. An important part of the cultural landscape must have been the tribal areas set up as administrative *civitates* and the development of *civitas* capitals. While the existence of the *civitates* of the Catuvellauni and Dobunni are not in question, even if their border is, it is hard to know how fragmented the previous social and cultural landscape was and therefore the effect of the road pulling them together. It is clear that the building of Akeman Street was responsible for the inter-dependence of the *civitas* capitals of Verulamium and Corinium from their independent status in respective river valleys. The position and function of the town of Alchester was possibly an extension of this Roman administration but without the other aspects of a *civitas* capital. However, besides the towns of Verulamium and Corinium, which are the result of the influence of many Roman roads, the main indication of populations adapting aspects of Roman culture is the litmus of the early villas.

THE DISTRIBUTION AND SITUATION OF THE VILLAS

The experience of the route of Akeman Street in this period, as seen by the traveller, has been detailed in the previous section. However, can we see how the settler, in terms of the villa owners and peasants, saw the adoption of another culture? It would appear that these sites began about AD 70-100 and being so early have usually been seen as a statement of membership of a new political order demonstrated through adopting, and adapting, a new lifestyle in very different domestic arrangements – the rectangular house with its rooms dedicated to specific functions. The villas do indicate a change in design to rectangular houses, although this does not necessarily mean social change, just a change in the shape of the structure. It is entirely possible that the activities of feasting etc., that gave elite status to individuals and families in the later Iron Age, continued into the early Roman period but in a different domestic setting (Black 1994). Most of these early villas have evidence for continuity of occupation with the later Iron Age, however, each has a different physical setting and in many ways this reflects the relationship of the site to the early *oppida*, and possibly also relates to power relationships with the Roman provincial government. Ditches remained in its uncomfortable and windy site and it may be that the owners wanted to keep their iconic position for display and demonstrate their continuing later Iron Age authority as well as their new affiliations. However, the orientation of the villa building is not what would be expected of an enclosure with its mouth facing east, so it is possible that it was no longer as intimately related politically to the Bagendon complex or the Welsh Way but towards the junction of the latter with Ermine Street. Ditches, being so close to the fortress at Kingsholm and the new power base that was developing at Corinium, may have felt it necessary to display itself to the new order, to be recognised as an active place of economic and political power in the face of their strength being eclipsed.

The distribution of the known early villas along Akeman Street is skewed heavily towards the Grim's Ditch enclosure, and considering the development of the Iron Age landscape, the existence of this heavily populated area may well have been a major factor in the road's course. There can be little doubt that the main cluster of villas within Phase Two of the Grim's Ditch was developed from this later Iron Age settlement pattern. There are a number of fascinating and provocative issues behind the location of this group of early villas. Phase Two of the Grim's Ditch only makes sense in terms of the cluster of high-status later Iron Age settlements and the development of the area from the elite ritual centre of Phase One which gave identity to the social group around it to the creation of a large enclosed area. Whether or not this reflects the beginnings of a change in identities, or a maintenance of them, is a difficult issue for which there is evidence on either side. The construction of the same earthwork profile of ditch, bank and palisade (a tempting, but unsupportable, argument is that the palisade was added later to the Phase One ditch system at the time of the construction of the second phase) indicates that there was continuity and this may also imply a lack of change in the social and economic relationships with in the area. Phase Two of the Grim's Ditch was not only a demonstration of status by the community that it enclosed and which was responsible for its construction, but also an indication that the Roman provincial government was comfortable with the political power of the road being 'compromised' by the enclosure. This situation is made even more intriguing by the area not becoming something more politically significant, such as happened in Silchester or Verulamium where the later Iron Age centres became *civitas* capitals in the Roman period. The continuing political uniqueness reflecting the identity and status of social groups in the area may well have resulted in its being outside the *civitas* of the Dobunni in which it is usually placed in the Roman period.

This does not mean that the population had no connection with Cirencester. Wilcote is just 37km from Corinium, a five-hour day at 36-45km by horse, as opposed to the 15-20km on foot with a beast of burden resulting in two days travel and this suggests that travellers using the latter form of travel were staying in the roadside settlements (both journey estimates gained from personal experience). Such a relationship with a major settlement such as Corinium could not have happened without shrinking the time/distance ratio. Although it might be an exaggeration to suggest that Akeman Street was built to join Corinium with the Grim's Ditch area, and to link the north–south Silchester to Towcester road to the enclave, the inhabitants of the Grim's Ditch may have had an important stake in the growing city, so much so that the Verulamium Gate was structured very ornately, a symbol perhaps not just of the town welcoming the incomers but the incomers paying for, or demanding, such a display of power. The fact that the villas remained invisible from the road throughout their lives indicates that the owners were comfortable with not having to, and had no need to, display their wealth.

Although Akeman Street was important politically the valley villas were situated according to the north–south trackways and the Evenlode as an important routeway. The connections between these clusters of settlement and agriculture can explain why the north–south routes remained so important in the early Roman period and beyond. North Leigh and Fawler appear to be the central sites, both on slight slopes above the Evenlode valley and facing towards it in a very similar manner to Ditchley's location in a smaller valley in the earlier phase. However, neither site can be seen from the road, both being hidden by spurs on the valley side, and both face towards the Evenlode, although neither site is visible from the other. It may have been fortuitous that the pre-villa commercially sited locations at both North Leigh and Fawler also faced a desirable 'Roman' landscape around them as the axis of movement within the area changed with the construction of the Phase Two earthwork. With valley-based trade communications it made more sense to demonstrate power through display on the more used routes, rather than on a road that may have had little traffic. Both the Ditches site and those within the Grim's Ditch demonstrate continuity, and indicated a need to remain an important part of the landscape through the identity and power of adapting new building methods. There was no need to flaunt power to outsiders in a politically secure environment such as the Grim's Ditch. That the Grim's Ditch villas were related to each other in some way can be seen by the presence of tracks in the present Wychwood environment which clearly join them. There are also routes that join the villas to the Thames valley settlements and it is tempting to think that villas within the earthwork circuit had their main lands and agricultural wealth in the Thames valley, with the lower Cotswold hills being a much more pleasant and impressive place to live. This has continued throughout the historic period with the large houses, Cornbury, Ditchley, Heythrop Hall and Blenheim Palace, being spectacular in the landscapes, and related to the Rivers Glyme and Evenlode, occupying sites close to important Roman villas and drawing their wealth from outside the area. The growing towns, Woodstock and Charlbury, as well as the villages, demonstrate the presence of this movement in the modern landscape. A curious issue is why there are so few known settlements or villas around Alchester and Bierton. This is an area deserving of fieldwork, as the implications of such a large area of land without high-status settlement would be rather unusual and significant. It may be that this area formed part of the *territorium* of Alchester, since, considering the status of the Grim's Ditch area, the land to the west of the fort(ress) could not be commandeered and remained a state territory. Even more strangely, there does not seem to be any later Iron Age settlement under the roadside settlements along the Alchester–Bierton stretch of a pre-Roman route, though this does characterise the roadside settlements which all seem to come into existence in the mid first century and have no earlier occupation under them, which must therefore be indicative of a contrasting mode of, and attitude to, movement through the landscape.

The situation of Northchurch and Boxmoor is totally different from the other area of early villas in terms of the valley siting with steep slopes to the north and therefore south-facing. It would appear that neither villa is closely related to an *oppidum* type of settlement, nor had a pre-Roman presence, as far as is indicated by present evidence, and both may be related to the heavy industry taking place in the valley at Cow Roast. Both villas must have been intimately related to the river, Boxmoor perhaps being at a point at the confluence of the Gade and Bulbourne, where transhipment of the smelted iron blooms from Akeman Street to the Gade and then south might have taken place. Boxmoor was also situated on the southern side of the river but in a location where the landscape was more open than further up the valley which incurred visual domination of the confluence at Two Waters. That there seems to be some sort of planning in the location of these structures is clear. Of the 8km or so between North Church and Boxmoor each building of the second century appears to be 2km apart. Another characteristic of these structures is that they face Akeman Street across the Bulbourne stream, and this is always the case even where the road changes sides of the valley to make its course more direct, indicating a determined effort to display. Boxmoor also had evidence of painted plaster of the quality that might be expected in later villas and the find of a seal indicates that the villa might have an imperial or provincial role. The possible navigability of the Bulbourne might have been a significant factor in the situation of the villas, particularly as iron blooms may have been transported south. This inter-visibility with the road is an important issue, since it meant that the road was directly opposite to where later Iron Age sites had developed.

There are clear cases that areas along Akeman Street might have been influenced by the early provincial government, however the many villas 'on top of' later Iron Age deposits indicate continuity and it is unlikely, though not impossible, that these sites became the homes or centres of estates for retired legionaries.

MOVEMENT OF CULTURE AND VILLAS

A number of the early villas along Akeman Street have similarity of design and appear to have been built over a period of perhaps 50 years. The Ditches villa might have been built to demonstrate a Roman veneer, not to Roman officials who might have considered the form of the 'row type' villa, the 'cottage' house, to be very basic, but to the local populace. Parallels with the Ditches villa include Boxmoor and Brixworth, the former on the route of Akeman Street, the latter near Towcester, well connected with the route; Park Street and Lockleys are also within easy reach of Akeman Street (Neal 1979). North Leigh, Shakenoak and Ditchley in the Grim's Ditch area may have similar arrangements of rooms and although it appears that they have shallow wings as part of their original design, the difficulty of determining plans from the publication of the former and the rather confused remains of the latter makes this uncertain.

What is interesting about these comparisons is that the designs are similar, but with variations, and their dates do also vary, so that when a winged corridor house is being built in one location along Akeman Street, another has a simple row house. Clearly, these broadly similar designs must have been carried as 'ideas' along Akeman Street. There are a number of prerequisites for adopting a design. First there has to be a need for such structures – individuals might not have needed to impress their subordinates or their neighbours, and it may be that this is what is happening at Barnsley with its late development. So if a villa-type building is seen as desirable and affordable, a design also has to travel.

It has been suggested that the 'row' and 'winged' corridor types of structure can be paralleled in Gaulish villas and, as has been suggested here, it might be that *oppida* were introduced by outsiders (a strong possibility is that they came from Gaul). If this is the case, when the elites of the *oppida* were ready to adopt Roman culture, a connection with Gaul would not be surprising. Whether the idea of the villa travelled from east to west or up the valleys from the Thames is difficult to know though the latter might explain the clustering in row and winged corridor types in specific localities. The excavators of Ditches thought that it may have been an outlier of the early building design. Milton Common has been seen as an exact replica of Ditches and although not on Akeman Street, would certainly have been influenced by the patterns of settlement suggested, with the Thames being the important cultural mobility route. However, it is worth looking more closely at mechanisms for the dissemination of any body of ideas. One is 'expansion diffusion' whereby 'the innovation grows in direct contact usually in situ, where an idea is communicated by a person who knows about it to one whose does not'. Then there is 'relocation diffusion' which involves the initial group of carriers moving, so they are diffused through time and space to a new set of locations (Humphreys 1988). There are similarities between town houses in Corinium and Verulamium villas later in the period, but at the time of the construction of the early villas, neither town had progressed so that the structures could act as a model for the villas. Black (1994) suggested that the early villa designs were similar to the *mansiones* of the Continent which may have provided a model for villas through the travels of ex-soldiers who had served in the Roman Army either early in the conquest period or even before. There is little doubt that aspects of the designs of these *mansiones* were similar to the row-type cottage villas, but rather than an idea that travels through location diffusion from another part of the Empire carried by returning soldiers, there was a model much closer to home in the presence of *mansiones* along Akeman Street. In terms of the Grim's Ditch there are the possible sites at Asthall and Sansoms Platt, outside of the area, and being official structures they may have had an important influence. The adoption of the design by the Grim's Ditch elites (and the Ditches' elites also) may indicate that there was no model in the towns. The use of the pattern derived from this source would also have been similarly developed in Gaul and therefore further explain the relationship through a common source. Also, if the *oppida* did have connections with Gaul through the original incomers, then the movement of ideas from that source may well explain the similarity of villa designs. Both expansion diffusion and relocation diffusion may well be working together in the villa designs.

TRADE

Evidence for trading along Akeman Street is sparse during the late first and early second centuries, and perhaps we should not be looking for the road as a facilitator of the Roman economy, but responding to local factors at different networks of trade at different times. For the period being focused on it is likely that elites were still maintaining 'traditional' values and were more concerned with the self-sufficiency of the estate and care for those within the hierarchical social system. Presumably, the army had to be supplied and there would have been some creaming of agricultural produce possibly by a site such as Alchester in all phases and shapes of its existence. With the growth of Cirencester and Verulamium, 'local' needed to become wider as interests in the town, as well as the supply of goods to the rural owners of a town house, expanded. Presumably, sites such as Asthall provided the negotiators who acted as middlemen for the movement of cattle and corn. It would have been easier for cattle to have been transported on the hoof, and therefore Wilcote, with clear signs of butchery, provided for very local consumption. Evidence from the use of Akeman Street for the movement of other goods is less prominent than might be expected. Pottery imports into

Corinium from the kilns in the Verulamium area in the direction of Akeman Street from *c*.AD 100/129 to AD 160 is about one to two per cent, and by *c*.AD 250-300 the Nene Valley was providing two to four per cent (Cooper 1989). Most of the other materials and artefacts were local or regional. The continued use of Cow Roast and the movement of iron would have remained important, but building materials at all the urban areas could be accessed locally.

The only two settlements along Akeman Street not at crossroads that have been excavated recently and with high standards are those at the villa at Shakenoak, and the small-town at Asthall, and an analysis of goods being brought into these settlements during *c*.AD 100-160 is informative (Booth 1997; Hands *et al.* 1972–8):

From distant sources

Iron and coal (Forest of Dean?) along Akeman Street from Cirencester
Bronze, silver and lead objects, brooches, tweezers, personal ornaments: local markets/travelling tradesmen
Glass beads: travelling traders
Pottery: Castor Ware, New Forest Wares, Severn valley, Black Burnished Ware 1, Rhenish Wares from Colchester
Sandstone Whetstones from Kent and Sussex
Millstone Grit from the Pennines
Lava Quern, Northern Ireland/Inner Hebrides via Bristol Channel and Cirencester/trader
Shale? Kimmeredge?
Tesserae from Chilterns

Overall, the impression is that the imposed direction of the road was not important in terms of trade. This may well be because if wealth was derived for many of the villas from the sale of bulky agricultural products to the military or civilian markets, then the selection of a location close to a water transport network, where distribution costs have been estimated at less than one fifth of those for land transport, is likely to have been significant, hence the importance of the Rivers Evenlode and Cherwell, both first order tributaries of the Thames, and the Ver (Greene 1986, 40). If the wealth of the villas in the Grim's Ditch area was produced in the Thames valley then the major trade routes would have been along the river itself. Apart from the pottery and stone products, other items could have been brought to the area by travelling salesmen on the less important narrower routes where there were small villages, as it seems unlikely that Asthall might have acted as a market for these types of items. Paterson (1998, 164) sums up the situation well, in that we should not be looking at the economy of the road but a network of micro-regional economies whose natural rhythms and structures were the result of local needs which in some periods became more closely linked with the wider world and a wider market for goods. Again, the same processes and chronologies might well be factored in with the location of religious sites along the road with small towns acting as local foci, but with others (Wood Eaton south of Alchester and Sansom's Platt) at times having a wider relevance, and perhaps the trade cycles with more travellers on the road encouraged the growth of these religious establishments.

of the provincial government related to ironworking and manufacture, or the migration of elites from the Prae Wood area with the change in the socio-political environment.

WAS ROMAN URBANISM A SMOOTH OR DISRUPTIVE PROCESS?

Two large urban areas were connected by Akeman Street – Verulamium and Corinium – and there are contrasting trajectories of development between them. The change from Verlamion to Verulamium was imperceptible with the later Iron Age and early Roman period providing an example of a very smooth process through the encouragement of the elites who attempted to emulate aspects of Roman lifestyle, and the policy of the Roman provincial governor not to interfere in this process of internally driven change continuing into the early AD 50s at least. The North Oxfordshire Grim's Ditch area never developed into an urban settlement. It may have been considered by the Roman administration that such a concentration of power should not be strengthened or perhaps its power persuaded the invaders that the area was best left as a self-administering area. Of course, this might have also have been because of its position midway between the other *civitas* capitals. It is highly likely that the elites within the Grim's Ditch would have played an active role in the development of Corinium, and Akeman Street would have been important in this process by shrinking the time/space ratio between the areas. At the present time it appears that the Bagendon '*oppidum*' was in fact more likely to be the estate of an elite group rather than having the wide trading connections of the other centres discussed above. The development of Corinium may well have been delayed by the fortresses at Kingsholm and later Gloucester, but also by the need to consolidate further territory west of the Severn to give a *civitas* an appropriate area to administer. Perhaps the site of the town was chosen and laid out by the provincial government using the site at Ditches as a legitimate forerunner. In this case the name of the town Corinium Dobunnorum could have indeed come from this settlement, the first part of the title coming from a woodland and ritual area close to Ditches. This idea is strengthened with the major trade route, the present Welsh Way, using the valley of the Bagendon Brook. The process of urbanism appears to have been smooth at Verulamium, but at Corinium it occurred later, indicated by the changing route of Akeman Street which was an important political factor in the support of the elites of the Grim's Ditch area. Becoming Roman could be a long process, taking longer at Verulamium than at Corinium, but the continuities of the former would have had important implications for a maintenance of identity and memory, whereas the latter might be seen as more problematic. In both cases, Akeman Street was an important catalyst in these urban areas' conception and development, and carried identities and memories as well as power and trade, all of which were highly connected.

DID THE MILITARY PRESENCE HELP OR HINDER TRANSFORMATION OF NETWORKS AND THE DEVELOPMENT OF TOWNS?

It is difficult to find substantial evidence for any more than a fleeting presence of the Roman Army along Akeman Street except for the Alchester base. The very early establishment of the Alchester fort(ress) indicates that there was something, or someone, whose power needed protecting or monitoring. The Alchester fort(ress) is an anomaly, with not as much known about it as is presented in interim reports and a great deal of speculation that must leave the range of dating uncertain. Rather than seeing the installation in simply a Roman context, with the army changing the nature of movement and mobility, the Alchester installation could be seen as being planted deliberately to ensure the continuation of movement and mobility of trade and exchange systems of an elite, of whom many had actully maintained contact with Roman influence for some time. It would not be surprising to find that if the gateposts dated to AD 44 belonged to an annexe, then the main military installation that they were an extension of was, at the latest, AD 43. Sauer was prepared to consider that Aves Ditch was a later Iron Age feature constructed with some form of Roman assistance, and evidence of a pre-AD 43 military presence has been found at Fishbourne on the south coast (an area which may have been important as having trading connections with the Alchester area). It would be very strange if Aves Ditch and the fort(ress) were not connected in some way. The early and temporary military presence at Asthall can be easily linked to the construction of Akeman Street or small units moving through friendly territory. Rather than being a 'territory-holding road' (Davies 2004) Akeman Street might be best looked at as a 'territory of friendly powers confirming road'. The idea of a *limes* is unlikely considering the lack of evidence for the presence of the army and the dates and duration of occupation of proposed forts along its route.

The Roman government was subtle in its handling of different peoples, and protection of trade routes is a two-pronged strategy: not only does it place the army in an important position – it is better to be in territory whose elite depends on trade for their wealth – but it sends out signals of protection and stability. Alchester may have existed for 20 years or so, but it is perhaps more appropriate to consider it as a locality which may have been occupied by troops on a number of occasions. If we are looking for a *limes* then perhaps the Boudiccan Revolt is the time to consider defence in depth, with forts at Alchester, Dorchester and Towcester, containing any growing aggression. Cirencester had the fortress of Glevum close by and therefore may have had a fort to comfort and reassure the population, as one of the disadvantages of a compressed time/space ratio is that news of disaffection could also travel quickly.

In terms of military influence on the growth of towns, there would appear to be only two cases where this is applicable. Alchester obviously had a relationship with the later town, though its founding date and function are difficult to know.

It may be likely that it continued to have some sort of official role related to the administration of the region due to its presence on the later Akeman Street (and Silchester to Towcester road). Although a military presence has been detected at Cirencester any fort in the area would have been so short-lived that it would be unlikely to attract a significant local presence resulting in the development of a *vicus*. It is also likely that any auxiliary regiment would also have had its own set of followers, especially common law wives and children, as well as traders, and this would provide for most of their needs. The possibility of the military influencing the origin at a distance has been explored above.

KEEPING OFF THE STRAIGHT AND NARROW

This book set out to explore a method of evaluating the effect of one Roman road, Akeman Street, in moving through the later Iron Age and Roman landscapes, rather than just examining the static aspects of surveying and engineering. The change from the bounded areas of the later Iron Age to what Laurence (1999) calls a Roman linear view of space has been seen to be demonstrable in the development of Akeman Street. The act of becoming Roman, the development of new identities for the elites, was dependent on the road that connected them to the towns where the stamp of Roman planning and its relationship to the province, and ultimately to Rome, was carefully orchestrated. However, the focus of the archaeologist or engineer investigating the relationship of the road to towns and villas, misses the point that the bounded configuration of spaces survived with its memories and identities throughout the period *c*.AD 10-160, and that even though the elite families in those areas might have adopted a Roman persona, when back in their traditional spaces the identities and memories of the local population were also shared by them, and it is through accepting this and exploration of the importance of the road as part of the wider landscape, and the wider landscape being part of the road, that the complex nature of the road be appreciated.

Did the contrasting patterns of movement between the later Iron Age and the early Roman period become increasingly complex because of the development of inter-regional networks? The evidence along Akeman Street indicates that largely life continued as it was. It seems unlikely that changes in identity due to the existence of the road affected most people. Even the elites with villas and town houses took time to adopt these forms of living, or rather the forms of architecture. Presumably, elites continued to be multi-members of groups, only this time there needed to be added the Romano-British constituency, and Akeman Street enabled that relationship to develop. One thing is certain, Akeman Street was not a later subsidiary road of little use but a vibrant route that reflected the nuances of becoming Roman, but this process did take time.

So, was it worth developing a fresh methodology to explore the significance of tracks and roads in the later Iron Age and early Roman period? Certainly the concepts of identity in the landscape recognised by looking at patterns of settlement have been useful, as were the ideas of interleaved chronologies and the landscapes that resulted in terms of memory and power. Was it important to have walked the road? In terms of making a specific journey, rather than simply using books and maps to make many inferred judgements, it was valuable in understanding the scale of vision from the road to individual sites, and from the sites to Akeman Street. This was particularly so in that my movement along the road gave me 'bearings' on sites from different points in the landscape as well as the distance and the terrain along its course. All of these experiences demonstrated how the landscape was connected to the road and how this sense of linear space was connected to the landscape. During the writing of this book I have been able to situate myself in these locales in a way that has given me a feeling of a lived-in and sensed space. I had never intended to be the first person to walk the road solo since, probably, medieval times or earlier. I simply wanted to know something about the landscape by forming a 'deep' map of the road that made me look either side of it, rather than keeping my head down and, since I had to make no decisions about my route, treated it as a power-walking exercise. Rather than Akeman Street being a straight line it is better compared to oscillations on a fluorescent screen reacting to the forces of memory, power and identity in the landscape, and producing very idiosyncratic and spiked tracks changing or continuing the frequency and intensity of its modulations through time.

MAPS

Reproduced courtesy of Ordnance Survey

Northchurch
Box Moor
Gorhambury
Verulanium

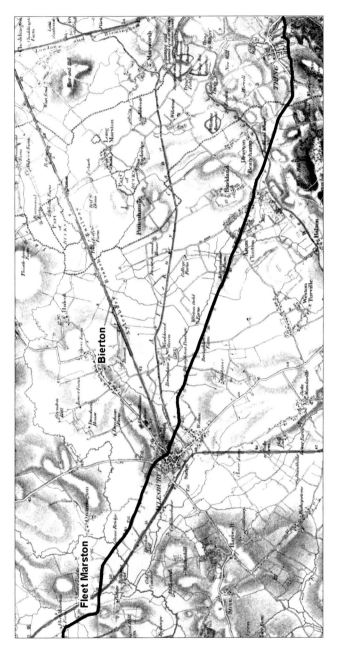

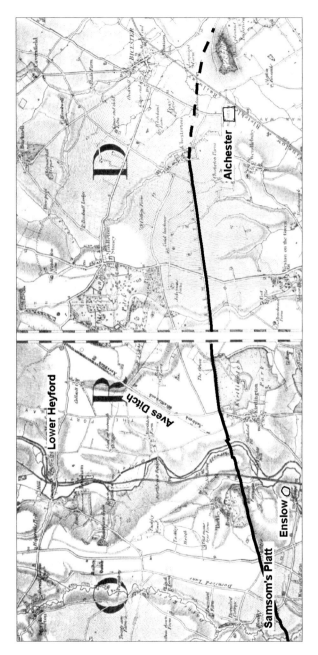

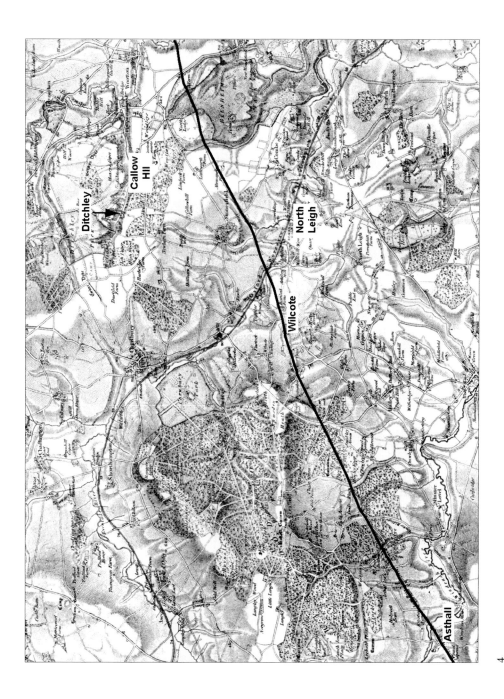

Ditchley

Callow Hill

North Leigh

Wilcote

Asthall

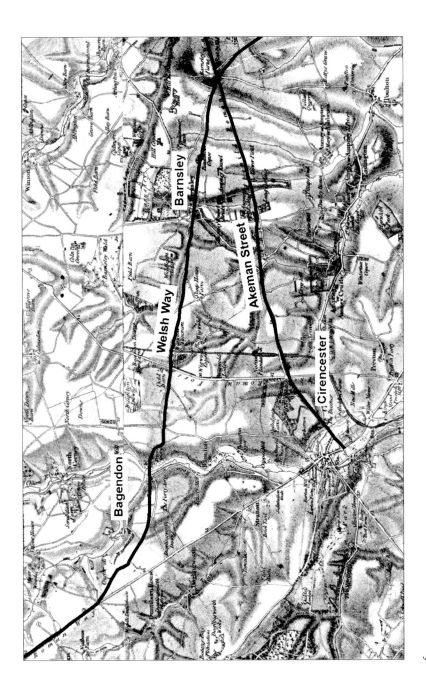

5

BIBLIOGRAPHY

IRON AGE AND ROMAN ROADS IN BRITAIN

Ainslie, R. (2005) 'Akeman Street – A Possible Roman Frontier', *South Midlands Archaeology* 35, 43-5

Bagshawe, W.R. (1979) *Roman Roads*, Shire Archaeology: Aylesbury

Codrington, C. (1905) *Roman Roads in Britain*, 2nd Edition, SPCK: London

Davies, H. (2004) *Roman Roads in Britain*, Tempus: Stroud

Forbes, A.F. and Burmester, A.C. (1904) *Our Roman Highways*, F.E. Robinson: London

Harrison, S. (2003) 'The Icknield Way', *Archaeological Journal* 160, 1-22

Johnson, D.E. (1979) *An Illustrated History of Roman Roads in Britain*, Spurbooks: Bourne End, Bucks

Margary, I.D. (1948) *Roman Roads in the Weald*, Phoenix House: London

Margary, I.D. (1955) *Roman Roads in Britain: I. South of the Foss Way-Bristol Channel*, Phoenix House: London

Margary, I.D. (1962) 'Roman Roads in Britain, their investigation and literature', *Archaeological Journal* CXIX, 92-102

Sherratt, Andrew (1996) 'Why Wessex? The Avon Route and River Transport in Later Prehistory', *Oxford Journal of Archaeology* 15 (2), 211-235

Shoesmith, R. (1990) *Alfred Watkin : a Herefordshire Man*, Logaston Press: Hereford

Taylor, C. (1979) *Roads and Tracks in Britain*, Dent: London

Viatores (1964) *Roman Roads in the South-West Midlands*, Victor Gollancz: London

Watkins, A. (1925) *The Old Straight Track*, Metheun: London

MOVEMENT, IDENTITY, LANDSCAPE AND TIME

Adams, B. (1995) *Timewatch: The social analysis of time*, Polity: Oxford

Aldred, O. (2002) *Historic Landscape Characterisation: Taking Stock of the Methodology*, English Heritage/Somerset County Council: London/Taunton

Allen, J. and Pryke, M. (1999) 'Money Cultures after Georg Simmel: mobility, movement, and identity', *Environment and Planning D: Society and Space* 17, 51-68

Cohen, A.P (1990) 'Self-Conscious Anthropology' in J. Okley and H. Callaway (eds) *Anthropology and Autobiography*, Routledge: London, 221-41

Edensor, T. (ND) *Walking through ruins*, Unpublished manuscript

Edensor, T. (2000) 'Walking in the British countryside: Reflexivity, Embodied Practices and Ways to Escape,' *Body and Society* 6 (3-4), 81-106

Fowler, P. (1998) 'Moving through the landscape' in P. Everson, and T. Williamson (eds) *The archaeology of landscape. Studies presented to Christopher Taylor*, Manchester University Press: Manchester, 25-42

Griffiths, J. (2006) *Wild*, Penguin: London

Ingold, T. (1993) 'The temporality of the landscape', *World Archaeology* 25, 152-74

Ingold, T. (2000) *The perception of the Environment. Essays on livelihood, dwelling and skill*, Routledge: London

Ingold, T. (2004) 'Culture on the Ground', *Journal of Material Culture* 9(3), 315-340

Johnson, M. (2007) *Ideas of Landscape*, Blackwell Publishing: Oxford

Jones, S. (1997) *Archaeology of identity: Constructing Identities in the Past and Present*, Routledge: London

Lee, J. (2004) 'Culture from the ground: walking, movement and placemaking', unpublished paper presented at the 2004 Association of Social Anthropologists conference, Durham: UK

Lee, J. and Ingold, T. (2006) 'Fieldwork on Foot: Perceiving, Routing, Socialising' in S. Coleman and P. Collins (eds) *Locating the Field: Space, Place and Context*, Berg, Oxford, 68-86

Long, R. (2002) *Walking the Line*, Thames and Hudson: London

Lucas, G. (2005) *The Archaeology of Time*, Routledge: London

Macfarlane, R. (2007,) *The Wild Places*, Granta: London

Petts, D. (1998) 'Landscape and Cultural Identity in Roman Britain' in R. Laurence (ed) *Cultural Identity in the Roman Empire*, Routledge: London 79-84

Riley, M., Harvey, D.C., Brown, T., and Mills, S. (2005) 'Narrating landscape: the potential of oral history for landscape archaeology', *Public Archaeology* 4, 15-26

Romey, W.D. (1987) 'The artist as geographer; Richard Long's earth art', *Professional Geographer* 39 (4), 450-456

Seamon, D. (1995) *A Geography of the Lifeworld*, Croom Helm: London

Sinclair, I. (2002) *Edge of the Orison: in the Traces of John Clare's 'Journey out of Essex'*, Penguin, London

Slavin, S. (2003) 'Walking as Spiritual Practice: the Pilgrimage to Santiago de Compostela', *Body and Society* 9 (3), 1-18

Soja, E.W. (1996) *Thirdspace, Journeys to Los Angeles and Other Real-and-Imagined Places*, Blackwells, Oxford

Tilley, C. (1994) *Phenomenology of Landscape: paths, places and monuments*, Berg, Oxford

Wallace, E. (1993) *Walking, literature, and English Culture*, Clarendon: Oxford

Wenger, E. (1988) *Communities of Practice: learning, meaning, and identity*, Cambridge University Press: Cambridge

Witcher, R. (1997) 'Roman Roads: phenomenological perspectives on roads in the landscape' in C. Forcey, J. Hawthorne and R. Witcher (ed) *TRAC 97 Proceedings of the Seventh Annual Theoretical Roman Archaeology Conference*, Oxbow Books: Oxford

Wylie, J. (2005) 'A single day's walking: narrating self and landscape on the South West Coast Path', *Transactions of the Institute of British Geographers* New Series 30, 234-47

VERULAMIUM, THE BULBOURNE VALLEY AND BIERTON

Branigan, K. (1985) *The Catuvellauni*, Alan Sutton, Stroud

Branigan, K. and Niblett, R. (2003) *The Roman Chilterns*, Chess Valley Archaeological and Historical Society: Chesham

Bryant, S.B. and Niblett, R. (1997) 'The late Iron Age in Hertfordshire and the Chilterns' in A. Gwilt and C. Haselgrove (eds) *Reconstructing Iron Age Societies Oxbow Monograph 71*, Oxbow, Oxford, 270-81

Bryant, S.B. and Niblett, R. (2001) 'The Late Iron Age in Hertfordshire and the north Chilterns' in J. Collis, (ed) *Society and Settlement in Iron Age Europe*, Sheffield Academic Press; Sheffield

Frere, S.S. (1985) *Verulamium Excavations. Vol 3* University of Oxford Committee for Archaeology Monograph 1

Haselgrove, C. and Millet, M. (1997) 'Verulamion Reconsidered' in A. Gwilt and C. Haselgrove (eds) *Reconstructing Iron Age Societies New Approaches to the British Iron Age Oxbow Monograph 71*, Oxbow: Oxford, 282-295

Hunn, J.R. (1980) 'The earthworks of Prae Wood', *Britannia* 11, 21-29

Hunn, J.R. (1992) 'The Verulamium Oppidum and its Landscape in the Late Iron Age', *Archaeological Journal*, 149, 39-68

Hunn, J.R (1995) 'The Romano-British landscape of the Chiltern dipslope: a study of settlement around Verulamium' in R. Holgate, (ed) *Chiltern Archaeology: Recent Work*, The Book Castle: Dunstable 76-91

Hunn, J.R. (1996) *Settlement Patterns in Hertfordshire: a review of the typology of the enclosures in the Iron Age and Roman landscape BAR British Series 249* British Archeological Reports: Oxford

Morris, M. and Wainwright, A. (1995) 'Iron Age and Romano-British settlement in the Upper Bulbourne Valley, Hertfordshire' in R. Holgate, (ed) *Chiltern Archaeology: Recent Work*, The Book Castle: Dunstable 68-75

Neal, D.S (1978) 'The growth and decline of villas in the Verulamium area' in M. Todd (ed) *Studies in the Romano-British Villa* Leicester University Press, 33-53

Neal, D.S. (1979) Northchurch, Boxmoor and Hemel Helpstead Station: the Excavation of three Roman Buildings in the Bulbourne Valley *Hertfordshire Archaeology* 4, 1-131

Neal, D.S. (1984) 'The shrine at Wood Lane End, Hemel Hempstead', *Britannia* 15 193-215

Neal, D.S., Hunn, J. and Wardle, A. (1990) *The Excavation of an Iron Age, Roman and Medieval Settlement at Gorhambury, St. Albans English Heritage Archaeological Report, 14* English Heritage: London

Niblett, R. (1990) *A Ceremonial Site at Folly Lane Verulamium Britannia Monograph no. 14*

Niblett, R. (1993) 'Verulamium since the Wheelers' in S.J. Greep (ed) *Roman Towns: the Wheeler Inheritance*, Council for British Archaeology Research Report 93, York

Niblett, R. (2001) *Verulamium*, Tempus, Stroud

Niblett, R. and Thomson, I. (2005) *Albans Buried Towns: An assessment of St. Albans archaeology up to AD 1600*, Oxbow Books in association with English Heritage: Oxford

Reece, R. (1985) 'The coins' in Frere, S.S. *Verulamium Excavations. Vol 3* University of Oxford Committee for Archaeology Monograph 1

Stead, I. and Rigby, V. (1989) *Verulamium: the King Harry Site: English Heritage Archaeological Report, no 12*. English Heritage: London

Thompson, A. and Holland, E. (1976) 'Excavation of an Iron Age site at Dellfield Berkhamsted', *Hertfordshire Achaeology* 4, 137-48

Zeepvat, R.J. (1997) 'The Roman Settlement at Cow Roast, Hertfordshire: updated project design and assessment report', Hertfordshire Archaeological Trust, unpublished report.

BIERTON AND AYLESBURY

Allen, D. (1986) 'Excavations in Bierton 1979: A late 'Belgic' settlement and evidence for a Roman villa', *Records of Bucks* 28, 1-115
Farley, M.E. and White, R.F. (1981) 'A Late Iron Age and Roman site at Walton Court, Aylesbury', *Rec. Buckinghamshire* 23, 51-75

ALCHESTER TO ASTHALL

Allen, T.G. *et al.* (1988) 'Excavations at Bury Close, Fawler, Oxon', *Oxoniensia* 53, 293-316
Atkinson, R.J.C. (1942) 'Akeman St. near Crawley, Oxon', *Oxoniensia* 7, 109-11
Booth, P.M. (1997) *Asthall, Oxfordshire: Excavations in a Roman 'Small Town', 1992. Thames Valley Landscapes Monographs No.9*, Oxford Archaeological Unit: Oxford
Booth, P.M. (1999) 'Ralegh Radford and the Roman Villa at Ditchley: A Review', *Oxoniensia* 64, 39-50
Booth, P.M., Evans, J. and Hiller, J. (2001) *Excavations in the extramural settlement of Roman Alchester, Oxfordshire, 1991 Oxford Archaeology Monograph No.1* Oxford Archaeology: Oxford
Chambers, R.A. (1978) 'The Archaeology of the Arncott to Charlbury Gas Pipeline', *Oxoniensia* 43, 40 -5
Chambers, R.A. (1981) 'Asthall', *CBA Group 9 Newsletter*, 11, 114
Copeland, T. (1988) 'The North Oxfordshire Grim's Ditch: a Fieldwork Survey.' *Oxoniensia* 53, 277-92
Copeland, T. (2002) *Iron Age and Roman Wychwood: the land of Satavacus and Bellicia*, Wychwood Press: Charlbury
Cotswold Archaeology (2007) 'Angelinos pumping station to Ardley Reservoir, Oxfordshire: Mains pipeline reinforcement. Post excavation assessment and updated project design for Thames Utilities Ltd' *CA Report*, 06058
Crawford, O.G.S. (1930) 'Grim's Ditch in Wychwood, Oxon', *Antiquity* IV, 303-15
Ellis, P. (1999) 'North Leigh Roman Villa, Oxfordshire: a report on excavations and recording in the 1970s.' *Britannia* 30, 199-246
Featherstone, R. and Bewley, B. (2000) 'Recent Aerial Reconnaissance in North Oxfordshire', *Oxoniensia* 65, 13-26
Fine, D. (1976) 'An Excavation on the North Oxfordshire Grim's Ditch at North Leigh', *Oxoniensia* 41, 12-16
Forster, A.M. (1989) 'Alchester, Oxon: A Brief Review and New Aerial Evidence', *Britannia* 20, 14-147
Hands, A.R. (1998) *The Romano-British Roadside Settlement at Wilcote, Oxfordshire. 1. Excavations 1990-92 BAR British Series 232*, British Archaeological Reports: Oxford
Hands, A.R. (1998) *The Romano-British Roadside Settlement at Wilcote, Oxfordshire. II. Excavations 1993-96. Oxford: BAR British Series 265*, British Archaeological Reports: Oxford

Hands, A.R., Broadribb, A.C.C. and Walker, D.R. (1972-8) *Excavations at Shakenoak I–V*, Privately Printed: Oxford

Hands, A.R. and Cotswold Archaeology (2004) *The Romano-British Roadside Settlement at Wilcote, Oxfordshire. III Excavations 1997-2000*, Hadrian Books: Oxford

Harden, D.B. (1937) 'Excavations at Grim's Dyke, North Oxfordshire', *Oxoniensia* 2, 74-92

Hargreaves, G.H. (1973) 'Roman Road System at Alchester', *CBA Group 9 Newsletter* 3, 18

Linington, R.E. (1962) 'Excavations at Lee's Rest, Charlbury', *Top Oxon* 8-15

Massey, R. (1999) *The North Oxfordshire Grim's Ditch: Cult, Status, Polity in the Late Pre-Roman Iron Age*, unpublished MA dissertation, Bristol University

O' Neil, B.H. St J. (1929) 'Akeman Street and the River Cherwell', *Antiquaries Journal* 9, 30-4

Radford, A.A.R. (1936) 'The Roman Villa at Ditchley, Oxon', *Oxoniensia* 1, 24 -69

Rahtz, S. and Rowley, T. (1984) *Excavation and Survey in a North Oxfordshire Parish 1970-1982*, Oxford University Department of External Studies: Oxford

Sauer, W.E. (2000) 'Alchester, a Claudian "Vexillation Fortress" near the Western Boundary of the Catuvellauni: New Light on the Roman Invasion of Britain', *Archaeological Journal* 157, 1-78.

Sauer, W.E (2005a) *Linear Earthwork, Tribal Boundary and Ritual Beheading: Aves Ditch from the Iron Age to the Early Middle Age.* BAR British Series 402, Archaeopress: Oxford

Sauer, W.E. (2005b) 'Inscriptions from Alchester: Vespasion's Base of the Second Augustan Legion (?)', *Britannia* 36, 101-33

Taylor, M.V. (1941) 'The Roman Tessellated Pavement at Stonesfield, Oxon', *Oxoniensia* 6, 1-8

Thomas, N. (1957) 'Excavations at Callow Hill', *Oxoniensia* 22, 11-53

Wilson, D.R. and Sherlock, D. (1980) *North Leigh Roman Villa*, HMSO: London

Winterton, H. (2001) 'A possible Small town at Sansom's Platt, Tackley, Oxon', *Britannia*, 31

Wilson, David R. (2004) 'The North Leigh Roman Villa: its Plan Reviewed', *Britannia* 35, 77-113

Young, Christopher J. (1975) 'The Defences of Roman Alchester', *Oxoniensia* 40, 136-70

BARNSLEY, BAGENDON AND CORINIUM

Baddeley, St Clair (1925) 'On certain minor ancient roads to and from Corinium (Cirencester)', *Bristol and Gloucestershire Archaeological Society Transactions* 47, 65-79

Clifford, E. (1961) *Bagendon: a Belgic Oppidum: A Record of the Excavations 1954-56* Heffer: Cambridge

Colyer, R. (1974) 'Welsh Cattle Drovers in the Nineteenth Century – 2', *National Library of Wales Journal* 18 (3), 29-45

Cooper, N (1998) 'The supply of pottery to Roman Cirencester' in N. Holbrook (ed) *Cirencester: The Roman Town Defences, public buildings and shops*, Cotswold Archaeological Trust: Cirencester, 324-41

Courtney, T. and Hall, M. (1984) 'Excavations at Perrott's Brook Dyke, Bagendon, 1983', *Bristol and Gloucestershire Archaeological Society Transactions* 102, 197-200

Cunliffe, B. (2003) 'Locating the Dobunni' in M. Ecclestone, S. Gardner, N. Holbrook and A. Smith *The Land of the Dobunni: A series of papers relating to the Transformation of the Pagan, Pre-Roman Tribal Lands into Christian, Anglo-Saxon Gloucestershire and Somerset*, Heritage Marketing and Publications Ltd.: Kings Lynn, 12-16

Darvill, T. and Hingley, R. (1982) 'A banjo enclosure at North Leach', *Bristol and Gloucestershire Archaeological Society Transactions* 100, 249-50

Darvill, T. (2003) 'The Land of the Dobunni' in M. Ecclestone, S. Gardner, N. Holbrook and A. Smith *The Land of the Dobunni: A series of papers relating to the Transformation of the Pagan, Pre-Roman Tribal Lands into Christian, Anglo-Saxon Gloucestershire and Somerset*, Heritage Marketing and Publications Ltd.: Kings Lynn, 2-11

Darvill and Gerrard, C. (1994) *Cirencester: Town and Landscape*, Cotswold Archaeological Trust: Cirencester

Hargreaves, G.H. (1998) 'The road network in the vicinity of Cirencester' in N. Holbrook *Cirencester: The Roman Town Defences, public buildings and shops*, Cotswold Archaeological Trust: Cirencester, 11-17

Holbrook, N. (2006) 'The Roman Period' in N. Holbrook, and J. Jurica, (eds) *Twenty five years of Archaeology in Gloucestershire. A review of New Discoveries and New Thinking in Gloucestershire, South Gloucestershire and Bristol 1979-2004*, Cotswold Archaeology and Bristol and Gloucestershire Archaeological Society, 97-132

McWhirr, A. (1981) *Roman Gloucestershire*, Alan Sutton and Gloucestershire County Library: Gloucester

Moore, T. (2006a) 'The Iron Age' in N. Holbrook, and J. Jurica, (eds) *Twenty five years of Archaeology in Gloucestershire. A review of New Discoveries and New Thinking in Gloucestershire, South Gloucestershire and Bristol 1979-2004*, Cotswold Archaeology and Bristol and Gloucestershire Archaeological Society, 61-96

Moore, T. (2006b) *Iron Age Societies in the Severn-Cotswolds: Developing Narratives of Social and Landscape Change*, BAR British Series 421: Oxford

Moore, T. (2007a) 'Perceiving Communities: Exchange, Landscapes and Social Networks in the Later Iron Age of Western Britain', *Oxford Journal of Archaeology* 26: 79-102

Moore, T. (2007b) 'Life on the Edge? Exchange, Community and Identity in the Later Iron Age of the Severn-Cotswolds', in C. Haselgrove and T. Moore (eds) *The Later Iron Age in Britain and Beyond*, Oxbow Books: Oxford, 41-61

Moore, T. and Reece, R. (2001) 'The Dobunni', *Glevensis* 34, 17-26

Mudd, A., Williams, Robert J., and Luton, A. (1999) *Excavations along Roman Ermine Street, Gloucesteshire and Wiltshire. The Archaeology of the A419/A417 Swindon to Gloucester Road Scheme*, Oxford Archaeological Unit: Oxford

Reece, R. and Catling, C. (1975) *Cirencester: Development and Buildings*, BAR 12, British Archaeological Reports: Oxford

Reece, R. (1976) 'From Corinium to Cirencester –models and misconceptions', in A. McWhirr, *Archaeology and History of Cirencester*, BAR 30, British Archaelogical Reports: Oxford, 61-79

Reece, R. (1990) *Cotswold Studies II: Excavations, Survey and records around Cirencester*, Cotswold Studies: Cirencester

Reece, R. (2003) 'The Siting of Roman Corinium', *Britainnia* 36, 276-80

Royal Commission on Historic Monuments (England) (1976) *An Inventory of Historical Monuments in the County of Gloucestershire. Volume I, Iron Age and Romano-British Monuments in the Gloucestershire Cotswolds*, HMSO: London

Sawyer, J. (1895-7) 'On some ancient roads in the Cotswolds', *Bristol and Gloucestershire Archaeological Society Transactions* 20, 247-54

Smith, J.T. (1985) 'Barnsley Park villa: its interpretation and implications', *Oxford Journal of Archaeology* 4(3), 341-51

Stevens, C.G. and Myers, J.N.L. (1926) 'Excavations on Akeman Street in Asthally, Oxon,

February-June 1925.' *Antiquaries Journal* 6, 43–53

Trow, S.D. (1982) 'The Bagendon Project 1981-1982: A brief interim report', *Glevensis* 16, 26-8

Trow, S.D. (1988) 'Excavations at Ditches hillfort, North Cerney, Gloucestershire, 1982-3', *Bristol and Gloucestershire Archaeological Society Transaction*, 106, 19-86

Trow, S.D. and James, S. (1998) 'Ditches Villa, North Cerney: an example of locational conservatism in the Roman Cotswolds' in K. Branigan and D. Miles, *The economies of Roman villas*, University of Sheffield

Trow, S., James, S. and Moore, T. (forthcoming) *Negotiating the Transition. Research and excavations at Ditches 'hillfort' and villa 1984-2006*, British Archaeological Reports British Series: Oxford

Wacher, J.S. and Pamment, S. (1998) 'The Town Defences' in N. Holbrook, (ed) *Cirencester: The Roman town defences, public buildings and shops*, Cotswold Archaeological Trust: Cirencester, 35-98

Webster, G. (1981) 'The excavation of a Romano-British Establishment at Barnsley Park Part I', *Bristol and Gloucestershire Archaeological Society Transactions* 99, 21-78

Witts, G. (1882) *Archaeological Handbook of the County of Gloucester*, G. Norman: Cirencester

IRON AGE AND ROMAN BRITAIN AND BEYOND

Allen, D.F. (1944) 'The Belgic dynasties of Britain and their coins, *Archaeologia* 90, 1-46

Allen, D.F. (1961) 'The origins of coinage in Britain' in S.S. Frere (ed) *Problems of the Iron Age in Southern Britain*, University of London, Institute of Archaeology Occasional Paper 11, 97-308

Black, E.W. (1994) 'Villa Owners: Roman-British Gentlemen and Officers', *Britainnia* 25, 99-110

Burnham, B.C. and Wacher, J.S. (1990) *The 'small towns' of Roman Britain*, Batsford: London

Burnham, B.C., Collis, J., Dobson, C., Haselgrove, C. and Jones, M. (2001) 'Themes for Urban Research, *c.*100 BC to AD 200' in S. James and M. Millett, (eds) *Britons and Romans: Advancing an Archaeological Agenda* Council for British Archaeology Research Report 125, 67-76

Collis, J. (1984) *Oppida: Earliest Towns North of the Alps*, University Of Sheffield: Sheffield

Creighton, J. (2000) *Coins and Power in Late Iron Age Britain*, Cambridge University Press: Cambridge

Creighton, J. (2006) *Britannia. The Creation of a Roman Province*, Routledge: London

Curteis, M. (2006) 'Distribution and ritual deposition of Iron Age coins in the South Midlands' in P. de Jersey, (ed) *Celtic Coinage: New Discoveries, New Discussions*, BAR International Series 1532, British Archaeological Reports: Oxford, 61-80

Derks, T. (1997) *Gods, temples and Ritual Practices*, Amsterdam University Press: Amsterdam

Green, D., Sheldon, H., Hacker, M., Woon, C., and Rowlinson, H. (1997) 'The distribution of villas in some south-eastern counties: some preliminary findings from a survey', *London Archaeologist* 8 (7), 187-95

Greene, K. (1986) *The Archaeology of the Roman Economy*, University of California Press: Los Angeles

Hingley, R. (1984) 'Towards social analysis in archaeology: Celtic society in the Iron Age of the Upper Thames valley 400 BC' in B. Cunliffe and D. Miles (eds) *Aspects of the Iron Age in Central Southern Britain*. Oxford University Monograph 2, 72-88

Humphries, M. (1998) 'Trading Gods in northern Italy' in H. Parkins and C. Smith (eds) *Trade, traders and the ancient city*, Routledge: London

Jones, B. and Mattingly (1990) *An Atlas of Roman Britain*, Blackwell: Oxford

Laurence, R. (1998) 'Land transport in Roman Italy: costs, practice and the economy' in H. Parkins and C. Smith (eds) *Trade, traders and the ancient city*, Routledge: London, 129-48

Laurence, R. (1999) *The Roman roads of Italy: mobility and cultural change*, Routledge: London

Laurence, R. (2001) 'The Creation of Geography: an interpretation of Roman Britain' in C. Adams and R. Laurence (eds) *Travel and Geography in the Roman Empire* 67-94 Routledge: London

Martins, C.B. (2005) *Becoming Consumers: Looking beyond Wealth as an Explanation of Villas Variability: perspectives from the East of England* BAR British Series 403, British Archaeological Reports: Oxford

Paterson, J. (1998) 'Trade and traders in the Roman world: scale, structure and organisation' in H. Parkins and C. Smith (eds) *Trade, traders and the ancient city*, Routledge: London

Taylor, J. (2001) 'Rural society in Roman Britain' in S. James, and M. Millett (eds) *Britons and Romans: Advancing an Archaeological Agenda. York: CBA Research Report* 125, 46-59

Thirsk, J. (2000) *The English Rural Landscape*, Oxford University Press: Oxford

Thomas, J. (1993) 'The politics of vision and the archaeologies of landscape' in B. Bender (ed) *Landscape: politics and perspectives* Berg: Oxford, 19-48

Trow, S.D. (1990) 'By the Northern Shores of Ocean. Some observations on accultural process at the edge of the Roman world' in T. Blagg and M. Millet (eds) *The Early Roman Empire in the West*, Oxbow Books: Oxford 103-8

Van Arsdell, R.D (1989) *Celtic Coinage of Britain*, Spink: London

Van Arsdell, R.D. (1994) *The Coinage of the Dobunni: Money supply and coin Circulation in Dobunnic Territory*, Oxford University Committee for Archaeology: Monograph 18

Walthew, C.V. (1975) 'The Town House and the Villa House', *Britannia* VI, 189-205

Webster, G. (1980) *The Roman Invasion of Britain*, Batsford: London

Welfare, H. and Swann, V. (1995) *Roman Camps in England: the field archaeology*. RCHME: London

Woolf, G. (1993) 'Rethinking the Oppida', *Oxford Journal of Archaeology* 12 (2), 223-34

Woolf, G. (1998) *Becoming Roman: the origins of provincial civilization in Gaul*, Cambridge University Press: Cambridge

Zanter, P. (2000) 'The city as symbol: Rome and the creation of an urban image' in E. Fentress (ed) *Journal of Roman Archaeology Supplementary Series* 38, 25-41

INDEX

Other titles published by The History Press

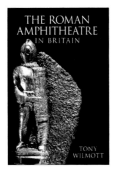

The Roman Amphitheatre in Britain

TONY WILMOTT

The first study of all the Roman amphitheatres in Britain, drawing on very recent excavations at Chester, London and Silchester. Tony Wilmott describes every amphitheatre, amphitheatre-type structure and mixed theatre/amphitheatre structure in the province. He discusses the different types - rural, military and urban - and the participants including the gladiators and animals. New evidence on the identity and behaviour of spectators is discussed. Illustrations include inscriptions, paintings, mosaics and artefacts.

ISBN 978 07524 4123 8

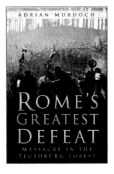

Rome's Greatest Defeat

ADRIAN MURDOCH

Over four days at the beginning of September AD 9, half of Rome's Western army was ambushed in a German forest and annihilated. Some 25,000 men were wiped out. It dealt a body blow to the empire's imperial pretensions and no other battle stopped the Roman empire dead in its tracks. Rome's expansion in northern Europe was checked. Drawing on primary sources and a vast wealth of new archaeological evidence, Adrian Murdoch brings to life the battle, its personalities, historical background and effects.

ISBN 978 07509 4016 0

Cartimandua: Queen of the Brigantes

NICKI HOWARTH

A unique insight into the life of this fascinating woman, Cartimandua, who was queen of the Brigantes tribe in Northern Britain in the first century AD. Little is known about the tribal ruler, who fought off rebellion and civil war and managed to keep her lands in the aftermath of the Roman conquest of AD 43. Her story is one of power, intrigue, scandal and accusations of betrayal and yet surprisingly she is a figure who is often overlooked and marginalised in studies of British history.

ISBN 978 07524 4705 6

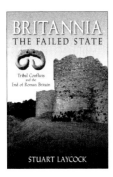

Britannia: The Failed State

STUART LAYCOCK

In this absorbing study Stuart Laycock explores the tensions and conflicts between the various tribal groupings that made up Roman Britain. He examines how tribal and political fragmentation could have contributed to the fall of Roman Britain and the immigration of the Anglo-Saxons. In a unique approach, this book analyzes Roman Britain, not as a unified entity, but as a collection of different peoples with a history of long term conflict, and finds parallels in modern conflicts.

ISBN 978 07524 4614 1

Visit our website and discover thousands of other History Press books.

www.thehistorypress.co.uk